Taking Measures

ALSO BY GEORGE BOWERING

Published by Talonbooks

And Other Stories (editor)
Baseball Love
Blonds on Bikes
Harry's Fragments
Kerrisdale Elegies
The Moustache: Memories of Greg Curnoe
My Darling Nellie Grey
The Rain Barrel
Sticks & Stones
Vermeer's Light
Writing the Okanagan

Taking Measures

SELECTED SERIAL POEMS

George Bowering

EDITED BY STEPHEN COLLIS

Talonbooks

Talonbooks
9259 Shaughnessy Street, Vancouver, British Columbia, Canada V6P 6R4
talonbooks.com

Talonbooks is located on xʷməθkʷəy̓əm, Sḵwx̱wú7mesh, and səl̓ilwətaʔɬ Lands.

First printing: 2019

Typeset in Arno
Printed and bound in South Korea

Interior and cover design by Typesmith
On the cover: *Untitled* XV, 2015, by Pierre Coupey. Oil on canvas, 102" × 222" triptych. Courtesy of the artist and Gallery Jones. Image credit: Ted Clarke, Image This

Talonbooks acknowledges the financial support of the Canada Council for the Arts, the Government of Canada through the Canada Book Fund, and the Province of British Columbia through the British Columbia Arts Council and the Book Publishing Tax Credit.

LIBRARY AND ARCHIVES CANADA CATALOGUING IN PUBLICATION

Title: Taking measures : selected serial poems / George Bowering ; edited by Stephen Collis.
Other titles: Poems. Selections
Names: Bowering, George, 1935– author. | Collis, Stephen, 1965– editor.
Description: Includes index.
Identifiers: Canadiana 20190088451 | ISBN 9781772012378 (HARDCOVER) | ISBN 9781772012446 (SOFTCOVER)
Classification: LCC PS8503.0875 A6 2019 | DDC C811/.54—dc23

For Jean Baird

Joy to the Spirit came,—

Such joy as when a lover sees

The chosen of his soul in happiness,

And witnesses her peace

—Percy Bysshe Shelley, “Queen Mab”

The Earth Poets

Who write small poems,

Need help from no man.

—Gary Snyder, “As for Poets”

Contents

Of the Dissolved
On George Bowering's Serials and Procedures

by Stephen Collis

1

There are poets who experience long and often difficult silences between bouts of feverish composition. There are also poets, versions of this first type, who, while always actively in pursuit of their work, find it a painstaking and time-consuming process of listening, gathering material, pondering, and patiently attending the moment when the words will come out just the way the poet wants. Sometimes these same poets are simply ruthless editors of their own work, who revise and rewrite the same few poems – or same few lines or even words – again and again and again, with microscopic attention, so that what finally finds its way into print (slight as it might be) is as compressed as diamonds. Then there are the polar opposites of these, poets who simply must write, compulsively, on a daily basis – improvisational language machines around whom the pages continually accumulate at breakneck speed, who simply cannot stop producing, for fear they will stop, once and for all. George Bowering falls into this latter category – is, perhaps, its paragon. A "Collected Bowering" would be a massive book – a multi-volume set of doorstops overflowing with six decades of continual, almost frantic practice. But if the book is to be contained within a single set of covers, the editor must make choices. There have been collections of Bowering's "best lyric poems," and selected volumes sampling his work across a range of forms and styles.[1] But to my mind his characteristic work has been in long serial and procedural poems: poems premised on the sort of ongoingness that best suits this poet's propulsive need to continue writing. *Taking*

Measures gathers material from the full range of Bowering's work in these longer forms, over an almost fifty-year period.

It is because George Bowering's long poems are so consistently located in proximity to the poet's lived reality – a poetry of actual, and often carefully documented, times and places of daily practice – that it is necessary to begin by separating the biographical poet from what Bowering came to call the "biotext."[2] "All writers keep a double in store," Margaret Atwood writes, "so they can save the reality for the art, and George's double was just more obvious than most" (Atwood 2014, 62). So obvious, he sometimes gets in the way of our actually reading what he has written. I like Atwood's inversion: the poet as false front for the "reality" of the art. The double Bowering kept in store for his "public life" is the affable prankster known to so many Canadian readers and writers. This is the Bowering who Rebecca Wigod describes, in *He Speaks Volumes: A Biography of George Bowering*, as a "capering personality, endearing to some, annoying to others" – the Bowering who was "the class clown as a boy in the forties and would still do anything for a laugh" (4). It is this George Bowering whose booming voice rings out at so many baseball parks and poetry readings – and it is also this George Bowering who has cut such a colourful figure in Canadian letters, from being a founding editor of the influential "poetry newsletter" *TISH* in the early 1960s, while still a student at UBC, to becoming Canada's first Parliamentary Poet Laureate. This George Bowering has published over one hundred books, a number of them winners of prestigious awards, his legendary prolificacy an apparent effort to eclipse "George Woodcock's record" (mclennan 2014, 32) – an extension, perhaps, of his obsessive interest in baseball statistics.

It is this "real," if highly performative, George Bowering that we can leave aside, as we take the measure of the "reality" he saved for his art, where a more interesting "supposed person" – as Emily Dickinson called the speakers of her poems – holds forth in the daily life of his poetry. This is where Bowering's concept of the "biotext" is so important, so much the matter of his decades-long practice in extended, book-length forms. "Autobiography replaces the writer," Bowering writes in *Errata*. "Biotext is an extension of him [*sic*]" (34). Biotext suggests a near overlap of life and writing – an almost material imbrication of the two. Joanne Saul, in *Writing the Roaming Subject: The Biotext in Canadian Literature*, describes Bowering's biotext "as a way of privileging literary form as the place where the writer of a specific poem or fiction finds him- or herself" (4). So the subject is "performative and in process within the text." "Rather than admitting a gap between self and the text," Saul continues, "the term 'biotext' foregrounds the writer's efforts to articulate his or her self through the writing process."

Bowering's serial and procedural poems are extended articulations of this writing self-in-process. But they are so by rendering the self simply one object among many others in the poem. As Bowering writes, having lit upon Richard Ellman's description of modernism as "the imaginative absorption of stray material," "Charles Olson saw the poet himself as stray material, as an object among objects, not the solution, but one of the dissolved" (*Errata*, 13). This is part of what makes Bowering's long poems so interesting: they are a "solution" in which the lyric, with its presiding subjectivity, is "dissolved" – a process which nevertheless leaves the "flavour" of the lyric (subject) everywhere present.

2

That poem-as-solvent has most often been called, since the middle of the previous century, a serial poem. Arriving as though in answer to William Carlos Williams's call for "a new form *before* a *new* poetry of any sort can be written" (Williams 1947–1948, 11), the serial poem was so named by Jack Spicer as "a sort of joke" description of the poetry – at once discontinuous and continuous, evincing a complex relationship between part and whole in an extended series – he and fellow San Francisco Renaissance poets Robert Duncan and Robin Blaser had begun to write in the 1950s (Spicer 1998, 52). In his 1965 Vancouver lectures, Spicer explains that the serial poem "has the book as its unit," that it "has to be chronological," and that it must essentially be improvised: "You have to go into a serial poem not knowing what the hell you're doing ... You have to be tricked into it. It has to be some path that you've never seen on a map before" (52–53). The structure is modular, with typically page-length unit following page-length unit until a book-length series is complete. It is also, in its improvised qualities, related to what Spicer called "dictation," a method of composition intended "to keep as much of yourself as possible out of the poem" (8). Bowering's version of this is the "dissolved" self, ideally present as nothing more integral to the poem than any other "stray material." Robin Blaser, glossing Spicer's comments on dictation and seriality, refers to a "practice of the outside": "A *reopened language* lets the unknown, the Other, the outside in again as a voice in the language" (Blaser 1996, 276).

In *How I Wrote Certain of My Books,* whose title pays homage to Raymond Roussel, Bowering notes that, by the 1970s at least, he was "leaning toward" the serial poem, towards a poetry "more likely to be incremental than expository in its ongoingness" (60–61). Later he notes again, speaking of the serial poem, "if I wanted my work to lean toward someone's it would be Spicer's" (122). *Autobiology* (1972) is clearly an exercise in serial form – perhaps Bowering's purest. But the two poems that precede *Autobiology* in the present volume also relate to Spicer and the serial poem. *Baseball* (1967) is, in Bowering's estimation, "not a serial poem, not a Spicer poem. There is too much plan for that" (*How I Wrote,* 21–22). That may be true, but Spicer's presence is everywhere in that poem – it is dedicated to him, for one thing – and it self-consciously takes the book as its unit of composition, as the majority of Bowering's long poems would.[3] Bowering had attended Spicer's 1965 Vancouver lectures; the "lean" in that direction had begun before any of the work collected here in *Taking Measures* had been written.

In commenting on *Genève* (1971) in *How I Wrote Certain of My Books,* Bowering mentions Spicer's own experiments with the tarot deck as an inspiration: "We were reminded by Spicer that the cards were there to help us bring the invisible into the visible world, not by reason alone but with the help of chance and nonsense, two things I was to look for in my tarot book" (35). There is a clue, here, to exactly what Bowering does with the serial poem. Ted Byrne, writing on *Genève* in *The Capilano Review,* notes that the serial poem is "not constructed according to a plan. It is made of a series of forgettings that persist and return" (Byrne 2014, 73). He goes on to explain that "Using the tarot procedurally to structure the poem may seem to contradict this description, but it actually introduces a complimentary element of chance." This "contradiction," this almost-but-not-quite a serial poem, becomes Bowering's hallmark, as his long poems are pitched right down the middle between the serial poem proper, with its unplanned and open-ended series of "forgettings" and what is sometimes called the "procedural poem," which employs various constraints to ensure the "complimentary element of chance"[4] – and perhaps avoid the attribution of the poem to the "subconscious."

Both serial and procedural forms of long poems work around the lyrical "I"/poetic ego by turning the poem's genesis over to various "outsides," whether they be the spontaneous dictations of suggestion – Spicer writes of "Martians" and radio waves – or the pressure of arbitrary constraint. Working with the tension between plan and spontaneity, between the serial poem proper and the procedure, Bowering takes up simple and often loose constraints and then lets happen whatever happens within the space of that constraint. *Genève* is thus generated by having each page of the series respond to a randomly chosen card from the tarot deck, page after page, until the last card is drawn. It thereby carries what Byrne calls "a narrative charge," but eludes "narrative capture" (Byrne 2014, 74) – "the reader finds no comfort in the series, no origin, and no closure" (79). The use of the tarot deck is a "procedure," but Bowering bends the procedure away from closure. This is typical of many of the series gathered in *Taking Measures*.

Allophanes (1976), for instance, with twenty-six numbered sections, was written while Bowering sat in on a Robin Blaser course on Yeats and Joyce at Simon Fraser University in 1974 – each installment of the poem written during one of the twenty-six lectures. Blaser's materials and words formed the constraint, while the poet sat, "pen in hand," he writes in *How I Wrote Certain of My Books*, "looking perhaps like any student making notes in his professor's lectures" (57). The sequence begins with a dictated line, the voice of Jack Spicer speaking directly into Bowering's "head" to say "The snowball appears in Hell / every morning at seven." Bowering sites Valéry's pronouncement that "the gods make you a gift of one line and it is your task as a poet to somehow not disappoint them with the next" (57). The "procedure," then, is the structure of the twenty-six lectures, with some of Blaser's words finding their way into what the poet writes. But the exercise is also one of dictation and automatic writing, as other elements enter into the page Bowering shapes during the lecture: random thoughts, bits and pieces from his own reading, observations, flights of fancy, misheard quotations, the given poem's own evolving momentum, and the poet's meta-commentary on the process:

> There is no perspective
>   when the eye is transparent
> When the author dies
>   I disappear
>
> Companionship is true growing up,
>   I reach for the companionship of art.

Blaser named other poets both "companions" and "horizons."[5] There are probably several companion-horizons present in Bowering's lines – Blaser of course, but possibly Emerson (that "transparent" eye), possibly Roland Barthes too (that dead author lying there). The serial poem, for Bowering – as it was in many ways for Blaser, Duncan, and Spicer – was to be an open-ended conversation with "the many co-workers in the great task of poetry" (*How I Wrote*, 42).

There are many other ways Bowering uses simple constraints to prime the pump of his serial poems – a "world of strange initiatives in poetry," as Ken Norris comments, "interesting strategies for writing book-length poems or serial poems" (Norris 2014, 65). Often the constraints continue to be about "companionship." *Irritable Reaching* (1986) – with its echo of Keats's famous negative capability letter – is a twenty-six-part alphabet poem, with each poem an acrostic of another writer or artist's name. The alphabet, Bowering notes, is his "favourite constraint," "because it was arranged in an order without any logic" (*How I Wrote*, 90). *Delayed Mercy* (1987) works with two main constraints: one is environmental, the poems being written at two in the morning, "when my poor brain would be at its most vulnerable" (*How I Wrote*, 96); the other comes back to the poetry of conversation, as each poem was written after reading an entire book of poetry, in one sitting, by another poet, who becomes the poem's dedicatee. Once again, the constraint is loose enough that Bowering can turn the poem in almost any direction, and the series can go on as long as needed with its – potentially at least – "unending design."

3

Spicer was not the only shaping influence on Bowering's early work on the serial poem; Gertrude Stein was also key. If the serial poem had to be written with the poet "not knowing what the hell" they were doing, Steinian automatic writing provided another appealing model. Reading Stein in Montréal in 1970, and taking his lead from Robert Duncan's "Stein Imitations"[6] and Duncan's embracing of the notion of being a "derivative poet," Bowering began his own imitations or "variations" on Stein's prose. *Autobiology* is an improvised and semi-automatic series of forty-eight prose "Chapters," which lean heavily on repetition as the poet reflects on memories grounded in his own bodily experience. For example, Chapter 45, "The Operation," involves the poet's encounters with the surgeon's scalpel:

> You bastard you bastard I said to my own body, part of my body I want you to hear about. It is my body & it rimes, this is the basis for composition & autobiology it is going to be there if you can hold still long enough for it. Hold still he said this is going to hurt & the water gusht out & a wave will cover the toes of your shoes if you stand still.

Stein's "Composition as Explanation" is the obvious point of reference here for Bowering's "composition & autobiology." Stein writes: "Each period of living differs from any other period of living not in the way life is but in the way life is conducted and that authentically speaking is composition" (517). The "way life is conducted" is what Bowering is most commonly attempting to embody in his serial poems, and in *Autobiology* that life is the accumulated experiences of the body, a self that is composed of experiential constituent parts and the text of this life – its "composition" – is similarly an accumulation of experiences grounded in lived time and place. Take, as another example, Chapter 1, "The Raspberries":

> I loved the way they were made of many pieces in my mouth, & they came from the outside of the bush & the inside. They came from the outside in the sunshine & from the inside in the darkness, & that is where they went again. But inside in the darkness is where we are told the subconscious is & that is why I could not eat raspberries.

The "subconscious" is materialized in the poem in the form of "a bug" that the young Bowering may have accidentally eaten along with a raspberry, thus bringing something "outside" "inside" the body, triggering a phobia: "I could not eat raspberries for years after that day." What is crucial for Bowering is not the nature of the subconscious, about which he is consistently dubious,[7] but the composition of the self via a series of discrete embodied experiences: the memory of the feeling of raspberries in his mouth, the possibility of having eaten a bug, the fact that things exterior to the body become part of the body, the accumulated series of such interactions composing a life. It is the series that is the point, "beginning again and again" in each lived moment, as Stein writes, "when there is a series" (Stein 1990, 516). The series embodies the simultaneous continuity and discontinuity of experiences – a series not encompassed by a linear "past present and future," as Stein again writes, but by a "prolonged" or "continuous present" (517–518). Bowering takes up this temporal problem, which he derives from Stein, in Chapter 35, "The Next Place":

> The next place is really a series of places so that the next place is really time, that is, a series, not as on the railroad, though that is certainly, there ... & though we thought we thought it was always different we always acted as if it was the same, perhaps, because we were, where we were, was always the same, though we spoke always of the difference, from time to time, of the place, & so, there you are. The next place, then, is always, a series of times, & we were always careful about time.

Time, Bowering concludes, "is converted into space." Time is not comparable to "the railroad," with a direction and constant movement, but is rather a spatially arranged series of "nows." Stein – who otherwise might appear to be a "presentist" – is actually in agreement: "The composition is the thing seen by every one living in the living they are doing they are the composing of the composition that at the time they are living is the composition of the time in which they are living" (Stein 1990, 516). The understanding of time both writers stake their poetics on – and I think it is worth being precise here – is, according to the philosophy of time, a "static" or "tenseless" theory of temporality, which "treats time a lot like space" (Bardon 2013, 87). Adrian Bardon, in *A Brief History of the Philosophy of Time*, describes "an array of timeless moments that are not only static but lack a direction," (122) an arbitrary series exemplified by the alphabet, one of Bowering's preferred structural devices for a poetic series. Essentially, this is time according to Einsteinian General Relativity.

Joseph Conti, in discussing the serial poem as the pre-eminent form of "postmodern" poetry, also makes the link to physics clear:

> the series articulates both the indeterminacy and the discontinuity that the scientist discovers in the subatomic world. The concept of serial form could not be convincing without the "granular" physics of subatomic particles and molecular combination and recombination. (Conti 1991, 19)

Bowering, I would argue, in his experiments with seriality and simple procedures for generating long-form poetry, is very much interested in avoiding narratives which might depend upon long standing "meta-narratives," while at the same time coming to grips with mortality and the anxiety produced by the – apparently – rapid *passing* of time.[8]

Nowhere is this more evident than in *Do Sink* (1992), "a sonnet's worth of sonnets," as Bowering describes the "crown" of fourteen free-flowing poems (*How I Wrote*, 130), each one an extension of one of the lines from Keats's "When I Have Fears that I May Cease to Be." Written while Bowering drove around rural Alberta in search of his maternal grandmother's grave, Keats's poem provides more than a "procedure" for Bowering to follow – it is a method for resisting the irresistible approach of death. Bowering *inhabits* Keats's poem, expanding it, slowing it down for frame-by-frame analysis. *Do Sink* is at once a gloss on Keats's poem and theme, an homage, and an act of remaking the poem in the image of Bowering's own poetics. It is also, arguably, one of Bowering's most beautiful poems.

When I have fears that I
may cease to be
open to pain that shines
wet on the side of a gold
fish in my own, I thought,
pond

        I ought to forget
comfort, forget family
history, drive a black sedan
over thin prairie roads
looking for a town even
my mother does not believe
was ever there

                knowing
pain is not colour, not value
but condition, the cost
of starting a damned life in
the first place, where no
thinking man ever was.

Conti, again, provides an excellent description of the serial poem's method here: "The predominant postmodern impulse has been not to destroy, or rupture, but to mutate and fuse as a process of 'making it new'" (Conti 1991, 10). In Bowering's words, his writing "takes its first foothold in previous writing, that I revise, imitate, contradict, embrace, renew" (Nichols 2014, 154). It is the process, again, of "derivation" – Duncan – and "dictation" – Spicer – that Bowering holds to throughout his long career; the work of prior poets is mined to produce the new work. It is a practice that blurs the lines between reading and writing, critical and "creative" procedures, allowing Bowering to be at once a loving "fan" of certain favourite authors – Stein or Keats – and a poet seeking his own place "in the tradition" (Nichols 2014, 154).

Arguably Bowering's most famous – and even outrageous – "derivation," as well as perhaps his most accomplished poem, is *Kerrisdale Elegies* (1984). In this case it is not an engagement with a beloved precursor – Bowering in fact admits that he "didn't like Rilke all that much," the poet was simply very much "in the air" in Vancouver at the time (*How I Wrote,* 85). Nevertheless, after a false start with a homophonic translation from the German, which he does not read, Bowering began a loose translation of Rilke's ten-part long poem *Duino Elegies,* working from a range of well-established

English translations. Bowering is not after precision: he takes liberties, foremost among them the "translation" of Rilke's poem's context from early twentieth century Europe to Bowering's own 1980s Kerrisdale neighbourhood in Vancouver, as well as the transformation of Rilke's "angels" into his own "spooks" or "ghastly dead". It is an audacious and unattributed theft (the poem's source in Rilke is unattributed) and – the great poetic sin – toys with being mistaken for a mere paraphrase of an original "masterpiece."

Duino Elegies is not a serial poem, but Bowering lays his elegies out as a series of nearly discrete page-poems, so there is yet another level of translation – that of poetics. Bowering stays close to Rilke's original, line by line, but constantly makes the poem his own, whatever that might actually mean in this context; as he does with Keats in *Do Sink*, he inhabits the original poem's themes and ideas, exploring them anew, providing a striking creative gloss and expansion. But where with Keats the derivation was one driven by a love of his precursor, here Bowering steps around Rilke himself, deriving directly from the language itself. Rilke, as a historical figure, does not matter at all to Bowering; he is simply a source of material, of an arrangement of language that Bowering can appropriate and rearrange. This "appropriation" could also be called a "commoning," as Robert Duncan writes in *The H.D. Book*: "The goods of the intellect are communal" and flow "from the language itself" (Duncan 2011, 546). "The English language," Bowering writes, in clear agreement with Duncan, "is a giant derivation machine" (*How I Wrote*, 43).[9] This is Bowering's approach across all his serial and procedural poems: listening carefully to the language itself – taking the material of poetry up *as material*, and *working it* – as the shaping *outside* within which daily life unfolds, and in which the poet's mortal singularity is *dissolved*.

4

The record of the poet's "life and times," framed as a series of discrete yet continuous temporal moments of "the way life is conducted" – the biotext that nevertheless gets "rid of the lyrical interference of the individual as ego," thereby revealing "secrets objects share" (Olson 1997, 247)[10] – Bowering achieves all of this largely through the simple "constraint" of a daily writing practice. There are "travel" poems which are fashioned by writing one segment of the poem each day of the poet's trip. *Blonds on Bikes* (1997), written while travelling in Europe, and *Los Pájaros de Tenacatita* (2013), written in México, are both composed this way; it is a process which highlights the conjunction of place and time – of fleeting moments of objecthood carefully observed and recorded. There is something about being away from home and normal routine that heightens the compression of life and work, as Bowering himself notes of *Blonds on Bikes*: “It’s almost as if living is writing poetry or *vice versa*” (*How I Wrote*, 134).

His Life (2000) takes the conjunction of the composition of one’s times and one’s poetry one step further, using the poet’s own journals as source material for a long series. Bowering began keeping a diary in 1958; in 1988, after thirty years of almost daily recording, he decided to try to compose a serial poem using the diary as a constraint. “Banality is all right,” Bowering writes, but while it might be “alright” for a diary, *His Life* compresses large amounts of material, with each poem summarizing a season-in-the-life, which keeps banality in check. Nevertheless, it is definitely the quotidian moments of lived experience that Bowering wants to prioritize. Take, for example, “Summer 1963. Vancouver”:

> *Am I the god?*
> *or does this fire carve me*
> *for its use?*
>
> The romantic poet falls back on intensity of feeling
> rather than striving for clarity & precision.
>
> He lies in bed till the jangling is gone from his head,
> then rises and begins a poem by natural light.
>
> He doesnt believe that man is a super creature
> exalting his soul over a world made of things
> transformed by the superior imagination.
>
> •
>
> A man is more interesting
> than man.
>
> Neither is true, both sound swell,
> god and fire.
>
> He loves the bush,
> not the voice in the bush.

The “world made of things” – “the bush” rather than “the voice in the bush” – is what Bowering traces from his journals. But the "things" that compose the poet's world are also textual "things," so this poem begins with a quotation from H.D.'s *Collected Poems*. *His Life* is filled with passages from H.D. – a poet who has long been one of Bowering's companions in verse. It may even be that, in pondering his own "life's work" in a reflective journal-poem like *His Life*, Bowering wanted the companionship of another poet's collected lifework. H.D.'s presence is also an opportunity to resituate his own practice of writing-his-reading, a move away from the "saying," as he writes in "Winter 1985. Vancouver," of his own earlier lyric poems to the "Later Long Poems," where "You Listen And Write." Furthermore, it is another "dissolution" of the self, whereby taking the measure of one's own life is dependent upon one's relation to another poet's body of work, a relation which calls Bowering's own sense of his poetic self to order throughout *His Life*.

I will conclude here with the poem that gives this volume its title – *At War with the US* (1974):

> There comes a time
> when we must
> take measures.

This is the entire first page of this serial poem. The "measures" being "taken" are complex and not at first obvious. Written in 1973, the poem addresses the winding down of the war in Vietnam, U.S. imperialism, and the bombing of Cambodia, as well as the poet's daily life as he sees his daughter Thea "off to her war called school." So one measurement the poem takes is that between a calm and ordinary life in quiet Vancouver and the machinations of global politics. Indeed, this is Bowering's most overtly political work, written with the political poetry of Shelley and Duncan in mind, peppered with quotations from Walt Whitman and Emily Dickinson, both writing during an American war. Somewhere behind all of this is the ghost of Canada's own "War Measures Act," invoked by Prime Minister Pierre Trudeau in 1970 during the October Crisis, as well as an anarchic refusal of the state – whether in the form of its militarism or educational commandments.

> & who are we
>
> The sheer
> intensity
> & numbers of their bombs—

they are trying to obliterate
measure, the inevitable measure

& making count of themselves

We help them count
one two three

They see their fear
walking out of the bush
four five six

The "measures" taken by states against both internal and external "enemies" are such that they can and too often do "obliterate" any other form of measure. In this instance, "measure" is like "value": the word can signify simply material "exchange value," but it can also signify those difficult-to-measure "values" that form the very fabric of a life. Bowering's poem stands for those more subtle measures and values, against those obliterating measures and values of states and markets.

The "measure" taken in *At War* is also the measure of the serial poem – still a form Bowering is learning to master at this point in the early 1970s. "All verse is measure," Williams wrote. "We may not be able to measure it, we may not know how but, finally, it is measured" (Williams 1947–1948, 12). Like a number of Bowering's serial poems, *At War* is written in a notebook chosen for the task, and in this instance, the last page of the notebook determines the last page of the poem: It is written, one poem a page, until the notebook is filled. Chance – the aleatory fact of the unpredictable number of pages in the poet's notebook – once again draws attention to Bowering's attempt to keep the open-ended nature of the series and the procedural constraint in active tension. To remain with the tension between chance and determinism, between page and series, between "the way life is conducted" and the temporally contingent practice of writing poetry – this is the measure taken by Bowering's serial and procedural poems. The serial poem is born of relativity – takes the measure of the relative, relational spaces it constitutes *as it constitutes it*. And while this may not be something the poet knows how to measure, in advance, finally, the life is lived, the poem written to its inconclusive conclusion, and the measure is taken.

A NOTE ON USAGE

The original terminology used in these poems has been retained, even where that terminology, for very good reasons, has changed in general usage over the past few decades. Thus the gender specific "man" used to denote humankind generally is retained, as in the line "Man is not except as he does." This decision is taken not out of some sense of the sacrosanct nature of the original, but in fact to retain this poetry's sometimes problematic "stance" and the privileges and prejudices of the period it was written in. No poetry escapes its times' uneven distribution of authority, advantage, and disadvantage. If the speaker of these poems sometimes strikes the contemporary reader as problematically unaware of his advantages and viewpoint, it is because the male poet of the 1960s, '70s, and '80s – and the white heterosexual male of European descent alone – had a particular licence that is only now slowly being revoked. This is poetry written as lived, with as little filter applied as possible; what we thus encounter, in part, is the entanglement of both a particular subjectivity and historically specific social structures. Equally troubling, the word "Indian" is also retained, as in the reference to Manuel Louis as "chief of the Indians around Oliver." In the late 1960s, coming from the pen of a settler poet, this would be fairly standard usage. Changing the word to the now more appropriate generic "Indigenous people" or, more specifically, the Syilx First Nation, would simply cover over the realities of settler/Indigenous relations of the period which boil over into the poetry, where a cosmic baseball diamond becomes the meeting point for settler and Indigenous players.

—Vancouver, April 2019

NOTES

1 *Changing on the Fly: The Best Lyric Poems of George Bowering* (Vancouver: Polestar, 2004); *Particular Accidents: Selected Poems*, ed. Robin Blaser (Vancouver: Talonbooks, 1980); *George Bowering Selected: Poems 1961–1992*, ed. Roy Miki (Toronto: McClelland & Stewart, 1993).

2 On the connection between the biotext and seriality, consider Fred Wah's comment in *Diamond Grill* that "a biotext, perhaps more than other literary genres, seems an innately cumulative performance" (Wah 1997, ix).

3 *Baseball* was originally published by Coach House Press as a slim, bright green, pennant-shaped triangle.

4 Joseph Conti, in *Unending Design: The Forms of Postmodern Poetry*, carefully delineates serial and procedural forms: "The series is determined by the discontinuous and often aleatory manner in which one thing follows another," Conti writes, while "procedural form consists of predetermined and arbitrary constraints that are relied upon to generate the context and direction of the poem during composition" (3).

5 "Image-Nation 5 (Erasure," *The Holy Forest* (Toronto: Coach House Press, 1993), 113.

6 Published as *Writing Writing: A Composition Book for Madison, 1953: Stein Imitations* by Fred Wah and Pauline Butling's Sumbooks in 1964.

7 "I believe in the idea of verse as given by an inspirer, muse or ghost or whatever, but not subconscious, though I can see how that would do it for some people" (*How I Wrote* 86).

8 "Apparent" because, according to the physicists, the static theory of time is correct, while the flow and "directionality of time is ... based on a mere convention as it arises from human psychology" (Bardon 122).

9 Another version of this is told by Aaron Peck, who found a second-hand copy of Clarice Lispector's *Stream of Life* which was once owned by Bowering, in which the poet has underlined and copied out the lines "language has *already said* everything" (Peck 2014, 193).

10 Bowering writes of looking "for other ways to generate texts without the interference of my will" (*How I Wrote* 96).

WORKS CITED

Atwood, Margaret. "George Bowering and *The Gangs of Kosmos.*" *The Capilano Review* 3.24 (Fall 2014): 61–62.

Bardon, Adrian. *A Brief History of the Philosophy of Time*. Oxford: Oxford University Press, 2013.

Blaser, Robin. "The Practice of the Outside." In *The Collected Books of Jack Spicer*, edited by Robin Blaser. Santa Rosa: Black Sparrow Press, 1996.

Bowering, George. *Errata*. Red Deer: Red Deer College Press, 1988.

———. *How I Wrote Certain of My Books*. Toronto: Mansfield Press, 2011.

Byrne, Ted. "Justice Is a Woman: Reading *Genève*." *The Capilano Review* 3.24 (Fall 2014): 73–79.

Conti, Joseph. *Unending Design: The Forms of Postmodern Poetry*. Ithaca: Cornell University Press, 1991.

Duncan, Robert. *The H.D. Book*. Edited by Michael Boughn and Victor Coleman. Berkeley: University of California Press, 2011.

mclennan, rob. "A Shelf of Bowering's Books." *The Capilano Review* 3.24 (Fall 2014): 32–33.

Nichols, Miriam. "George Bowering and the New American Poetry: A Conversation." *The Capilano Review* 3.24 (Fall 2014): 148–154.

Norris, Ken. "Bowering's Books." *The Capilano Review* 3.24 (Fall 2014): 64–68.

Olson, Charles. "Projective Verse." *Collected Prose*. Edited by Donald Allen and Benjamin Friedlander. Berkeley: University of California Press, 1997.

Peck, Aaron. "On Nuts and Other Editions: The Books in George Bowering's Study." *The Capilano Review* 3.24 (Fall 2014): 193–196.

Saul, Joanne. *Writing the Roaming Subject: The Biotext in Canadian Literature*. Toronto: University of Toronto Press, 2006.

Spicer, Jack. *The House That Jack Built: The Collected Lectures of Jack Spicer*. Edited by Peter Gizzi. Hanover: Wesleyan University Press, 1998.

Stein, Gertrude. "Composition as Explanation." In *Selected Writings of Gertrude Stein*, edited by Carl Van Vechten. New York: Vintage Books, 1990.

Wah, Fred. *Diamond Grill*. Edmonton: Newest Press, 1997.

Wigod, Rebecca. *He Speaks Volumes: A Biography of George Bowering*. Vancouver: Talonbooks, 2018.

Williams, William Carlos. "A New Line Is a New Measure." *The New Quarterly of Poetry* 2 (Winter 1947–1948): 8–16.

The Way It Is with Me

by George Bowering

The first long poem I ever wrote was about headhunters in Malacca. I started it in high school and carried it for years, occasionally showing it to girls and then young women with a hope of appearing interesting. Finally, I lent it to an exotic female friend of my first real Vancouver girlfriend. That exotic young woman kept it for a long time, and eventually married a good friend of mine who happened to be a poet. I have no idea whether he ever got to read it, and I never saw it again, thank goodness. Everything turned out well for all three of us.

I like that story, and it is close to true. I think that what I lent to Dolly was really my first short story, "My Brother's Keeper." So, if I were now writing a note for my partly collected short stories, I would just have to change headhunters to brothers, and it would be true. Or close. In any case, I am happy to report that neither the long poem nor the story has shown up, as far as I know.

Before I went to university, I liked realism, in fiction and in poetry. I wanted to write like James T. Farrell and Kenneth Rexroth. I wanted to pursue facts and thus reality. It took a while, but I learned instead to pursue the poem, to try to go where it was going.

It was very romantic, going to university. You could go into a big stony library and read all the books you wanted – for free. So I decided to read the books of poems that were labelled "PS" something, U.S. poetry. Some "PR" along the way, a bit of "PQ." It was difficult but romantic to go through Hart Crane again. It was an enjoyable slog through Whitman. There wasn't much H.D., but it was better than the few tiny lyrics in the anthologies I'd seen.

Then one afternoon I pulled out a newish volume titled *The Desert Music,* and started to give it a little read. Time became tempo. It was all at once closing time in an empty library. I was standing with sore legs on the bottom tier, and when I dropped the book from my sore hands it made a very loud echoing clatter on the concrete floor.

That was the moment I felt that I could learn poetry. William Carlos Williams was an old man when he made that beautiful long poem, and would wind up saying "I am a poet." But he also said (and you could not stand between the stacks and not move your lips while reading):

> I am that he whose brains
> are scattered
>   aimlessly

It would be years before I learned that he was semi-quoting Goethe. It was enough to hear for the first time how rime works when someone frees it.

So I grabbed all the Williams books I was allowed and took them to my rented basement with the cot and plywood desk in it, and started reading all those little doctor poems – I'd found my realist poet.

Then I tried to read *Kora in Hell.* And whatever strange classroom I had looked into, I wanted a seat in it. Many years later I sat in on a semester's lectures by the great poet Robin Blaser, and wrote a poem (*Allophanes*) all the while he was talking. But Dr. Williams – he started it for me. He wrote an early poem addressed to his old mother, a poem in fifteen sections. Here is the fifteenth:

> All this—
>   was for you, old woman.
> I wanted to write a poem
> that you would understand.
> For what good is it to me
> if you can't understand it?
>   But you got to try hard—
> But—
>   Well, you know how
> the young girls run giggling
> on Park Avenue after dark
> when they ought to be home in bed?
> Well,
> that's the way it is with me somehow.

So it's been with me, I think. I love both difficulty and seeming simplicity in verse. What I am not fond of are laxity and self-expression. So you see why I keep mentioning William Carlos Williams and H.D. and Jack Spicer.

Whoever was handing out good luck, I'd like to say thanks for seeing that the wonderful little magazines and innovative poetry presses arrived just in time. I owe my soul to the poets and other angels who found space for us at Talonbooks, Coach House Press (and then Coach House Books), El Corno Emplumado, Véhicule Press, Black Moss Press, and others. They say you make your luck. I don't know. I just wanted to write a poem.

—Vancouver, April 2019

Baseball

A Poem in the Magic Number 9

Vancouver and México City
1965

(Coach House, 1967)

for Jack Spicer

The white sphere
turns, rolls
in dark space

the far side of one destroyed galaxy,
a curve ball
bending thru its long arc
past every planet of our dream.

A holy spectre of a curve ball,
dazzling white, brand new
trademark still fresh
"This is a regulation Heavenly League Baseball"

O mystic orb of horseshoe stitching!
Hurled from what mound in what Elysian field,
        from what mound, what
        mystical mount,
                where what life-bringing stream?

God is the Commissioner of Baseball.
Apollo is the President of the Heavenly League.
The Nine Muses, his sisters
the first all-girls baseball team.
Archangel Michael the head umpire.
Satan was thrown out of the game
for arguing with the officials.

In the beginning was the word, and the word was
"Play Ball!"

Now that white sphere
cools,
and the continents
rise from the seas.

There is life
on Baseball.

The new season is beginning.
Zeus winds up to throw out
the first ball
like a thunderbolt.
Take me out
to the ball
game.

July in Oliver, cactus drying
in the vacant lots,

in the ball park, the Kamloops Elks
here for a doubleheader, Sunday

baseball day in Oliver, day of worship
for me.

At the park an hour early,
scribbler full of batting averages,

sometimes I got a steel basket
and sold hotdogs, peanuts, sometimes

I picked up a broken bat, lugged it home
and taped it, not so much for batting

as for my collection. Louisville Slugger.
My father was official scorer,

high in the chicken wire box
on top of the grandstand, he was tough

on the hitters, as later I was,
pens and pencils in front of me. Oliver

nearly always won, the cars parked
around the outfield fence honking

for a hometown rally, me quieter,
figuring out the percentage, a third the age

of the players, calculating chances
of the hit and run play.

Later,
I was official scorer, they knew

I had the thick rule book memorized.
Sweat all over my face, eyes squinting

thru the chicken wire, preparing
batting averages and story for

the *Oliver Chronicle.*

Manuel Louie, old Manuel Louie
is chief of the Indians around Oliver.
1965 now, he is 94, but he looks 55.
He's still got big black mustache, shoots pool
with his belly hanging over the rail.

Age 80, he was still playing Indian baseball games,
the chief, bowlegged running bases with turkey feather
in his hat.

The Wenatchee Chiefs, class A,
were spring training in Oliver then,
letting Manuel Louie work out at shortstop, weird Sitting Bull
Honus Wagner,
in exchange for his steam bath, that's how he looked 40
at age 80, a creek beside his house, mud hut full of steam.

That year the Wenatchee Chiefs finished fifth.

The New York Yankees
are dying this year, the famous pinstripe uniform
covered with dust of other ballparks.

Mickey Mantle is a tired man with sore legs,
working at a job. Roger Maris forgotten
on the sports pages, a momentary spark
turned to wet ash.

A beanball on the side of the skull
killed a ballplayer
when I was a kid,
it was violence
hidden behind the grace of base-
ball.

Now Warren Spahn is trying
to win a few more games
with his arm 44 years old,
in the National League
where no pitcher's mound is Olympus.

And Willie Mays is after all
sinew and flesh
as a baseball
is string and leather,

and when baseballs get old
kids throw them around,
torn horsehide flapping
from that dark sphere.

I was in love with Ted Williams.
His long legs, that grace,
his narrow baseball bat
level-swung, his knowledge of art,
it has to be perfect, as near
as possible, dont swing
at a pitch seven centimetres
wide of the plate.

I root for the Boston Red Sox.
Who are in ninth place.
Who havent won since 1946.

It has to be perfect.

In the nineteenth century
baseball came to the Pacific Northwest.

Mustache big muscled ballplayers of beer barrels
among bull lumberjacks and puffsteam train engines,
mighty trees of rainforest, pinstripe uniforms,
those little gloves of hurt hand, heavy bats of yore,
baseball in Seattles and Vancouvers of the past when Victoria
was queen of Canada, Manifest Destiny of the ballpark
cut into the swathe of rainy fir trees.

Now still there—I go to see the Vancouver Mounties
of minor league green fence baseball playing
Hawai'i of the Pacific, Arkansas Travelers of grey visitors garb,
I sit in warm sun bleachers of behind first base
with Keep-a-movin Dan McLeod, bleach-head poet of the Coast
gobbling crack shell peanuts—he's sitting beside me,
gadget bag full of binoculars and transistor radio, tape recorder,
cheering for the Mounties, nuts, they are Dominicans of the North,
dusky smiling on the lucky number souvenir program,
where I no longer write mystic scorekeeper numbers in the little
squares,
sophisticate of baseball now, I've seen later famous players here.

What you doing, they ask,
young esthete poet
going to baseball games,
where's your hip pocket
Rimbaud?

I see the perfect double play, second baseman in the air legs tucked
over feet of spikes in the dust, arm whipping baseball
on straight line to first baseman reach, plock of ball,
side's retired, the pitcher walks head down quiet from the mound.

The herring-
bone stitching
takes one last
turn
till Louisville Slugger
cracks
and the spin
changes, a cleat
turns in the
sod, digs earth,
brown showing
under green,
bent knee takes
pressure.

Lungs fill
with air,
pump-
action legs, foot
pounds on narrow
corner of the bag, rounding,
                the body leans
                inward, eyes
                flick up once
                under cap, head
                down, legs running,
                buckle!

and the fire that breaks from thee then told a million
times
      since 1903,
      the first
      World Series, white sphere
      turns, the world again
      spun around once, the sun
      in October again sinking
      over the pavilion roof
      in left field.

This story is for you, Jack Spicer, who had eyes to see
a small signal
from the box
              more than 90 feet
              away.

When I was 12 years old I had a baseball league
made of a pair of dice, old home-made scorebooks,
National Leagues, American Leagues, Most Valuable Players!

The St. Louis Browns played the Chicago Cubs in the World
Series!
The Yankees finished in seventh place, the batting championship
went at .394. It was chance, roll of the dice, blood doesnt tell
in that kid's bedroom season—

I was afraid to try out
for the Oliver junior league team,
I would strike out
every time,

till I was 16,
oldest you could be, and played
one game before my summer job,

and I hit a bases loaded single
in the first inning. I was the
tallest kid on the team.

But I bought *Sport Magazine* and *Baseball Digest,* and knew all
the numbers. Ty Cobb's lifetime batting average was .367,
I remember now, Rogers Hornsby's lifetime batting average was .358.
In 1921 Babe Ruth hit 59 home runs.

Ty Cobb was better than Babe Ruth.
Ted Williams was better than Joe DiMaggio.
I like the Boston Red Sox who are in ninth place.

I still play that game, I think.
I'm sitting at my desk in my bedroom right now.

Nine.
Is a baseball number.
Nine innings.
Nine players.
Ted Williams was the best hitter of all time.
And the number on his back was nine.

Here is today's lineup:

lf	Terpsichore
2b	Polyhymnia
rf	Clio
1b	Erato
3b	Urania
cf	Euterpe
ss	Thalia
c	Melpomene
p	Calliope

A lineup like that is enough to inspire
the faithfulness of any fans of the good art
of baseball.

I have seen it happen
to the best poets
of this summer
and last.

Long shadows
fall across the infield
in the ninth inning.
Sometimes ball players
look like they're dying
as they walk off field
in the dusk.
I knew an old man in San Francisco
came to life
when the Dodgers were in town.
Now he is dead, too,
and Jack is dead,
and the soldiers play baseball
in Asia,
where there is no season,
no season's end.
"It's just a game,"
I used to be told,
"It isnt whether you win or lose,
but how you
play the game."
In baseball
that is how you say
the meek shall inherit
the earth.
September 30, 1965,
Willy Mays has 51 home runs,
grey hair
at his temples,
he says he has been
getting tired
for six years.

I know I feel my own body
wearing down,
my eyes watch
that white ball
coming to life.
Abner Doubleday
lived in the nineteenth century,
he is dead,
but next spring
the swing of a
35 ounce bat
is going to flash with sunlight,
and I will be a year
older.
My nose was broken twice
by baseballs.
My body depends on the game.
My eyes
see it now on television.
No chicken wire—
it is the aging process.
The season
cant help but measure.
I want to say only
that it is not a
diversion of the intelligence,
a man breathes differently
after rounding the bag,
history, is there such a thing,
does not
choose, it waits and watches,
the game
isn't over till the last man's
out.

Genève

Montréal
July 5, 1969–February 8, 1970

(Coach House, 1971)

HE LOOKS ANGRY & too big for his horse,
pulling the head back & to the side,
his club held, a gnarld chunk of tree,
but there are no trees on the hill
he appears to protect.

What, is that me he holds, not horse,
but tree, I've so often calld myself?
Can I be the flourisht weapon & anger
of some club-man, some uniform
in this picture red & blue?

While bushes underfoot stand in peril
of being smasht into hoof-markt dust
that mad man will create & protect
for my loneliness?

SHE KNEELS at water's edge
not to draw but to pour it into the lake,
    water—does it come endlessly
from her two earthen jugs

    as the stars above her
include her head in their circle? Endlessly,
    her naked breast in line
with the pitcher she tilts
    that star-water from, silent lonely
& capable smile on her face.

    She is no mother of mine,
this woman with fleshy knee on earth,
    she is the eighth star
of a circular heaven, & not weeping

    but caring for a future, a general
thirst, all her men-children their
    cleaning, their taking for granted,
& she is the granting, the star
of ablution & drink,

                    this is how
the heavenly light of the night sky
    enters all our blood, what care!

THE MONARCH looks like a successful poet
bored with the even weight of his crown,
the baton held only by habit

while his eagle squats before him,
only a bird on the ground.
What sadness
on their faces, or what heaviness of the sea
they must support,
how changeless
that ever-changing weight!

His cheekbone leans on his hand,
his elbows on a rock,

his eagle is made of brass.

I have never liked that number five
or the V those emperors calld it.

I fear always that victory
above those rounded boulders.

HE IS LIKE ME, holding the sword
not to fight, but to deliver it
to one who knows he wants to use it.

Or for a moment he feels its balance, &
enjoys the craft

knowing this esthetic
is at the base of Hideo Kobayashi's equivalent
of soldier & artist.

He has his back turnd
to the white mountains
& brings his stylish dress
to some city on the plains
where the plumage of his cap
will serve him
as it retains its bright hue

& the other hand is knuckld at his hip,
a learned stance, as his mustache
is waxt,

his eyes wide open,
filld with expectation, rimmd with fright.

THE LION he wrestles with
could be made of bronze
or the papier mâché of heroic Italian films
we feed our empty spines upon,
that nervous
extension of our dreams.

How well this goes
till we can let the club lie on the earth
& splendidly meet the beast
with our bare hands.

That they be bare, that they bear
no fabrication, no matter how primitive
is no, not our strength,
but our grace, that
which endears us to our spectators.

I another Samson striding into
the enemy's camp, emboldend
by my picturesque victory
over the lion?

How I put my chin to his head
for leverage, how I first
broke his lovely limbs
& then his life!

Now my own foot looks like his muscld cat's foot.

My hair grows about my shoulders like a mane.

His lolling red tongue
in my mouth
serving his fiery red eye
in my forehead.

IS HE OFFERING the flagon
or preparing to leap head-first into it?
totally foreign to me,
an auslander's mind of strange japes.

But I see the cup's form
is repeated by the powder horn
or only military voice,
of the hunter
—either way a killer.

His horse is dainty in his beauty
stands only lightly on the earth
ready to spring at a sound

& I will not take offer of drink.

Looking closer again I see his leg
is seemly in its caressing of his animal,
his skirt as if toucht by wind.

I know the cup contains poison
only for me, his stranger;
his fierce eyes
are fed by that brave libation.

(THEY COME AT ME as over a hill
one by one, with weapon
or gift),

this one
with powerful thighs, horseless,
holding a stave taller than himself.
his hat removed, the plumage
hanging down

as if to shame me for my fear.

Maybe to lower my defence?

The thighs are muscld from long walking
but there is no path behind him.

(How many are they?
Is it my mind
throws up these apparitions,
that they
present their similar faces
& regular oddments
for my confusion

from which I should learn?)

What?

That I have fears & curiosities,
that with each turn of the wrist
I confront the present.

I learn to create the past
I live in.

If this man put on his hat
he would be tall as his staff.

(& YOU KNOW ALL ALONG it's myself
I'm talking about,
that discovering
you're so wise about,
I must walk
my own allotment of steps)

as this one's horse is prepared
to do so strikingly,
his hoofs raised
like the man's sword,

another weapon, held
this time as I might dream my grip

prepared

like a right cross

or the cross of his sword's singing
for a lost god-man
somewhere not beyond that
rise of ground.

He wears a small pistol too,
as decoration

or sign that his blade is not
a sharpness of confidence.

This is no boxer, but a minion
of his orthodoxy.

WHY SHOULD I TRUST this one
simply
because he has no horse? It's the fear

gone—this one behind a table
where he displays objects
for conjuring tricks.

Why trust him?

It is not trust but relief,
the rod he holds is no brutal weapon
but a wand,
for mercurial gesture.

His face is made to look like a child's,
that guile, that jester
fooling with my timid heart.

(How they
set me up, first the horseman, then
this creature ready to turn my money
to water in my hands.

Still better this fear
slipping in, than the flinching for
bloody death.

Rather personal loss to usury
than the streets of New York
with their staves.

Business-man or magician
I'm yet open to your thrust.

(IN THE OTHER DREAM assault
they are continually
stepping into water.

Here they surmount
a dry hill.)

This time though, I am offered the chalice
as in a toast
or tribute, the ceremonial
stick held softly against his shoulder.

Are there no women
in this apparition? Or women
only disguised as these
bearded creatures?

His animal has been transformd into furniture
indoors, cloven hoof on the lifted floor.

As the man wears his crown,
so his legs are twice covered—
no attraction there.

The chalice resembles his crown
at whose level it is held.

He is a sad weakling
old monarch. He offers me no fright,

& clearly

the cup is empty.

MY COLOUR by the stars
is sky blue

& he hangs against no sky
but a white ground

between trees
broken for this purpose.

I feel the blood rush to my head
in moments, hands hidden from help,
a story I have to tell,
the work of outside hands
seen in the twist of this thong

& the neck.

That suspense
turns me upside down till I'm caught

till I know turning away from the dark
depends on my body alone, to

clear the mind.

He may have been put there
for his clear mind, there

may hang a tale.

THIS ONE LOOKS as if he could kill me
with gentle fright,
    with propaganda from my home village
    & its 350 sunny days a year.

I never carried a book for outdoors
    as these child lovers do.
    The sun wouldnt let me look
    at the white pages.

          They are looking rather
into each other's eyes, where
    the eye of the universe shines forth.

    & the book forgotten among their coupld hands
    is only the light of reason.

The mountains are a distant horizon.
You dont have to look up to see them.
(as I did)
The sun fills the sky with his face.

         My friend Roy
         has written a small book
         about last weekend

         when he swallowd the sun
         & his face shone
         with bright eyes all over.

The sun isnt looking at the lovers.
It's looking at me.
It allows me to look at the lovers.

It uses its patient time
    above the clouds
        over the far mountains.

(I RETURN HERE after five weeks
still looking for these
pictures of a year)

to find the dark one with horns
holding his cat-like hand
over a weeping woman,
her face hidden in her palms.

She sits not in fright
but resolvd anguish
the other side of his hoofs.

His tail is turnd
to obstruct our view
of his cock

but that is what the woman
hides her face from
& we have his red ears,
the twin curvd red spikes
of his fork.

& the bush behind him
is lavish,
the green
is lavish,
the woman

no longer sees the abundant bush.

She hasnt yet seen me.

WHY THE HOUSE OF GOD
should be struck by lightning.

He does it himself, acting at times
like a poet, to kill
what he makes
in order to make,

those bodies
falling from disaster
are actors as well,
to be moved

to gravity & death. We should all
be ready to feel our weight.

Making a marriage, too,
as Paul had it   emblem of
a God's creation
& binding
made not too strong
that it can not be
shatterd by the
luminous arrows of heaven we inhabit

with our rarest minds.

The falling bricks
catch that light
& scatter it
into new configurations

half random, but toucht
with art.

I COULD PLAN more, I could
get ready for them
as they come over their hill.
I could arrange their order,
or predict their form-
ation.

But I'm rather surprised
to see this one sitting
on a chair presumably hidden
by thick folds
of his blue raiment,

royal, crown on his head,
wand bespeaking resolvd
power,
the two-coloured baton
held by his familiar hand
that shows pink

from ready armour
under the cloth.

He seems to be resting
momentarily, on his throne.
His sense of order
acts more sure to his mind
when he sits a horse,
moving men among blood
& moving the blood
inside his own manliness.

He sometimes has to predict
law in the quiet of this room
for signing papers. That is
his less welcome command.

(I MAKE NO ASSUMPTIONS
about their meanings,
they
are such strangers to me; seeing them,
I will tell what they look like,

not in circles
but over their hill, me
the horizon.)

This one *is* an emperor, more than king,
bearing a pendant from some far province
of a beast that appears
to be a bison.
But this is perhaps
four hundred years ago,
what country
is that?

His bare belly is muscular & creast
with expectant posture.

I see all that
metal on him, gold belt, red buckler,
domed & Christian crown, *etc.*

& think
where has all this gone? not rare metal
to museums,

but the meanings.

HE IS NOT LIKE ME. He carries the long sword
as if recently used, or ready for use,
like a professional

as I try to carry
a baseball glove, dangling from my hand.

& his pride
is upright, while mine is loose,
trying to appear that American, that
black, American genius to appear
loose as a black man.

This one sits on his horse
& looks to his right
with anger or anticipation
as if ready to kill another black man.

He's a knight
with long mustache, appearing German,
that stiffness, that pride in stiff
destruction, that
disguised skill to
strike swiftly, athletically,
as in movies
of German storm troopers speeding thru a town.

I hate this man
as much as I can hate an apparition;

he is so far out of my time
& place.
There is a path
behind him.

I KNOW THESE WARRIORS are familiar to some.
To Robin Blaser,
                    but he is gentle
on the gentle coast of this country. Who here
may make the introductions?

                                        To turn me
right-side-up again
                      in their fierce eyes?

         Or the foreign demonic eyes
         of this lady with golden wings?

               She pours from pitcher to pitcher
         a stream imitating the earth's gift
         of water behind her.

                                      Her hidden breasts
          uneven, no stream there now.

                         (What does an angel do
                                 with breasts?)

(or: who are you?)

                    Her muscular legs
                    speak of walking or age.

      Is she temperate in using those wings?
                    As I would be, my sin
                    not to use the feathers
                    grown from my own torso?

Her skirt leans the direction the tree leans
yet she never spills that water.

    Those wings like the lion could be bronze.

HE'S A LONELY MAN
with a long face
& his robes
ungainly

so far from his youth
he might have been
one of the warriors

this hermit, hidden away
save the light
of his lantern
I see him by.
His heaviness belies
the long thin face,

he carries as I do,
as I guess I'm part
of the looking now, wanting to say "we"
earlier, "we see him"
—that
must be the secret purpose of his hermitage.

"As if to shame me for my fear"
that I cant rest my mind's hand
on his simple walking-stick,
that I demand the sun
at times more dim
than his
candle encased
in bronze & glass.

HOW ODD
BENEATH THE MOON should be
that primordial creature
with mechanical parts
to reach & pinch;

the moon should roll
like a woman with her clothes off.

As if to show
that while the moon shines &
there is no time for battlers,
the primitive fighting beast
merely lies in shadow
beneath the lovers
& their music.

The work of outside hands,
crab-like at the lute,
or hers
extended from the balcony,

lookt over by that female face,
are only caught in time this night.

They must give away
to the majority.

But the scene is filld with leaves,
& these hard dark windows
are in shadow

while the crusty red animal sleeps.

SHE IS PINCH-MOUTHT
as if holding in   or ready to spout
            opinion

& anger.

The staff in her hand
is no penis, it is a woman's weapon

& the dress nearly falls
from her tits.

What can I make of her? This woman
promising a fuck
& a smash on the head?

Whatever make of them all
(as we make all of them)—

She is, after all, a queen
& we
must be subject.

She
is object

by virtue of the force promist
by her readiness
to do violence.

But I began
by naming the mere
aspect of her mouth

My staff will never comfort me,
my queen.

(NOW THE WOMEN are appearing
or are they as they would appear
only men in skirts & jewels?)

This imperious one sits
as in a wind, her brown hair
pickt up lightly, leaning
toward her staff of office.

Her other hand lifts one finger upward
as if pointing to her coronet

& behind her, on her throne
two craven acorns—

Nuts & staves.   Still she is lovely
& her breasts are two
& the strings of her beads
on her bodice.

Her body is swathd
in robes presumably imperial.

The symbols are difficult to
assimilate, as I wait
to find her womanness
appear.

An apparition I wait for within.

ROY IS COVERED with baubles,
all colours, red jewels
around his neck, red crown
on his long thick blond hair,

sitting on a curious eagle
throne, he displays
what seems a gold flower plate.

(Come on, George, you know the real name, see,
you dissemble already—)

But this royalty
I cant respect, especially sitting.

In school
I was expelld for "sedition."   How
can I even name his awe, this mere
hairy king?

(That is the fear made subtle, George,
ask Roy,
who dissembld even in
the midst of his vision, even
in his poem—)

At least this overdresst monarch
shows you his beauteous, empty,
platter,

the coin of his realm.

WHO IS THAT OLD MAN
watching the lovers? He
is friendly looking
or perhaps scheming, he
is perhaps a principle
dresst in an old man's rags.

They dont seem part of me at all,
the babe with the bow
is a familiar convention, never real

save later,
the pain of his arrow.

(I speak from the wisdom
I desire,
& the knowledge
of its despair.)

But the lovers stand
as in a dance,
facing an audience,
their backs to the weapon of love,
ready, those poseurs, but

She has her hand on his back
as she does,
that thing a man little expects
& loves, so.

HERE'S THE MOST MARTIAL, the most
powerful body of them all;
love
is vanquisht, lovers killed in a moment,
the moon itself scatterd
by this visage.

He rests so uneasily
on his chair, he looks about to destroy.

He is the purchast soldier
king.

(While these pictures fall
one by one, the walls
do not fall.)

I say that
out of this fear, this manufacturd
resentment of such power.

He holds a long sword as a woman
holds a phallus,
& his golden armour
is topt by a dangerous crown,
itself a weapon.

His eyes are on the sequesterd
lovers'
wall.

I COULD HAVE BEEN ONE
time imagining all this
lying in the sun at Big Sur
real as you can be, but.

I look in the mirror he holds
& see flowering, he is
towering over
the green bushes behind him,
overpowering
the mirror, a giant coin
of what realm?

He is one of the few
not glowering
from his force.
That force, a weakness
I may overturn with a
turn of the wrist.

What then of my fear?
The mountains are
a distant horizon
I may step over
to walk away
from them all.
Always
walking toward.

I am imagining all this

real as I can be.

His grip is gentle
on the disc, gentle
as the flowering
of his soft hat.

SHE IS THE POWER woman
attended by the brilliant peacock.

What world is this she holds her staff upon?
She is all pride
                to the reveald thigh, all
muscles that would make a lion
cringe.

              I come back to the bird.
              His colours seem only a grant
              from her power.

              She is no mother to him.
              His sex is controlld
              as his tail
              held parallel to the ground.

They are looking to the advance
              of some foe or petitioner
or they assume their agreed-upon pose
              of ownership over the land.

              Her eyes are not foreign, neither demo
They are relaxt in their home.
                                I flower
not like that bird, holding a paycock
position,
        yet seek no power
                              from woman
or my own plumage.

                        That I would fear,
that power,
              or hers.
                        Or the orderliness
of the bird.

SHE IS THE SWEETEST young girl,
a mad queen, holding up her wealth,
a plate
of gold.

(I call them plates
though I know *denier*
is not to eat from)
She's back
in this poem.

An antic one, she
doesnt know how to carry
her birthright.

So I love her
as I reach back into my days
on the sun's platter,
that gold.

She stands awkward
as if shy to take a stance.
The sceptre is correct
but her head held awkward
& the coin of her realm
wide open
to the sun's rays.

Beneath the loose red blouse
her breasts
are heavy
with no support
save her sweet muscles.

The muscles beneath my skull

respond,

répondez.

SO MANY WOMEN, so many functions
all disguising the one
disguisd finally in the man's
mind.

As this one carrying an immense goblet
proffers what appears an emptiness.

Her crown sits with assurance
on her head,
her knees make a slight ripple
in her skirt,
her fat face seems again
demonic.

Who drew this card?

I would never look into those eyes,

but that is not woman.
I would never
find courage to wrest the fancy stick
from her hands.

Seeing the huge cup in her hands
with no fluid to reflect her mad eye
I would turn heel & run.

THE JUDGMENT, YES, but why
this early or
why this late?

I'd always wanted it
at all points, an energy
toucht & touching back,

afraid to be naked as I was.
Naked as these forms rising from the earth
are.

The wingd child with
horn to his mouth
is not enough, is not
knowing enough.

Who's to judge? Who's to
sound the horn? Does this stranger
know the key I've always playd in?

Three of these people look at each other.
The fourth looks upward

None of them is I.

No one knew which way I was looking.

& now, not even I.

DO I ASK THE MAN in the warlike crown
to take me away in this chariot?

(I ask questions now, always
asking questions,
the chariot
being pulld two ways,
in a Y.

But Why?)

He's as if an interlocutor, in a drama,
the curtain pulld away to reveal him.

I am the audience.

But the chariot is drawn
toward me.
Who
draws this chariot?

I'm making pictures myself,
my own horses certainly
a fearsome power,
pulling in that Y.

(a letter
deliverd to the dead letter office.)

Looking again I see
no one in the driver's seat.
That
may answer that question, leading

beyond the twenty-fifth letter
to the ampersand
at the end.

ONE is sitting on top.
One holds to him, looking down.
One falls face forward into the abyss.
One stands blindfolded & turns
The Wheel.

Beside a bush of beautiful
red roses—oh fortune

so pretty in men's eyes
as the wheel begins
its upward turning
so slow.

Blindfolded, naked,
she turns the wheel,
but blinded & naked,

is that her fortune?

What does
is done to.

Who turns
will fall
with each weight
of the wheel.

Who will not sit astride the wheel
is already in the abyss,
eyes blinded.

A large black X is affixt

where he was fool to look,
the man at the top of the turn

& next to fall, where X
markt his spot.

WHY WOULD THE FOOL
wear such knowing face,

or what face
do they see on me,
in my motley?

But back, done tempt your self so
to your
self,
always that.
He holds two fingers
up, the first & fourth, the furthest
from one another.

Ah, ah, looking
too hard, looking for it, being

the unexpected,
unwanted kind of fool.

Begin once more with what you know
is a flute held against his cheek,
but to be honest with your eye,

it looks at first like a weapon.

But the two portions of his hat
droop with bells on the ends,

no horns inside them.

I'll never know what to say about him,
try desperately as I may
toward this end,

fool.

I'D FORGOTTEN TOO MUCH about it, till
here it faces me unexpectedly,

the World.

A bull,
a lion,
two ornamental birds, & one
vicious,
& a naked woman,
surrounded by
leaves & berries,
in a circle,
tied
with a red bow.

It was all there with me,
but I thought I'd broken all circles
running in rings myself,

never fearing the lion,
never facing the bull.

Free as a bird
who must kill, eat, & die.

Poison berries,
did I tie them so sweetly?

(But she looks so happy
standing before me, the usual
blue cloth held before her;

does she secretly
converse with those mighty
beasts?)

THIS LADY HOLDS THE SWORD

not as cutting weapon
but sceptre, a
symbol of power or grace.

Another monarch, the sexiest
yet,
her other hand held palm outward

to calm
or to ward off.

A pretense of vulnerability
it appears.

Her breasts are symmetrical,
the circles of her eyes
promise no violence,

she carries calm
even as her crown.

The short German skirt
is decoration,
another symbol.

She is the symbol
woman.

I dont need symbols. I

want that other naked one, the world

of berries & lions.

So it goes, so
it is gone.
So I enter here,
myself drawn.
not as blade or picture

but blood gone from the face.

ON THE DAY I HAVE THREE TEETH REMOVED

I encounter this young man
        walking with featherd hat in hand
& offering a giant cup
        seen to be empty
or just ceremoniously fed with some unseen fluid.

But what is that? He is no dentist
        & not the young hero
in my dream, escaping the dogs
        on snowshoes.

                Waking from the gas
I felt myself imprisond
        by a trio of charlatans,
one removing my teeth.

                I have no choice
to spit that part of me into the cup.
        It is gone,
                lifelong bone
into some
            earth's cavity on its way to river
& sea.

        I'd give my eye teeth

        to see where the cup is offered.

I ALWAYS LOOKT only for justice
& thinking I would offer justice,
never gave it at all.

Suspecting who comes behind her
I fear her sword
more than her scales.

Why
does she wear armour
beneath her loose robes?

Why
did the deep drug
draw my fear & distrust
& effort to free myself from my tormenters,

Why
will this woman
fall in a moment into uncontrollable tears?

Why
is her right knee flext
below the sword in her right hand,
ready to strike?

What have I opend
to her eyes
these thirty-seven pictures?

Who
is behind her?
Who
placed him there?

AS I FEARD the skeleton with the scythe
is the last one to appear

to me with no lyric in my throat
to be cut away,
                    no red smile
for you, but these dry bones
to clatter against those
if he will take me.

It was in the cards it should end with him.
What else could fall?

I will never enter the cool dark room
of that house far behind the edge
of the desert.

                    He is there to cut me off
curiously resembling a rock-ribd defenceman.

His number is thirteen.

Mine is presumably
up.
                              Already in his smile
                              he has more teeth than I do.

His weapon
goes against my grain.
                                I ask for no more
than two minutes

for one chance to score
                                a power play goal.

The lovely ladies, naked & robed & armourd,
may one last time cheer my fire
as I move my own blades over
then fall forever to the ice.

Autobiology

London, U.K.
June 12, 1970

Vancouver
June 12, 1971

(New Star, 1972)

CHAPTER 1: THE RASPBERRIES

When I was thirty I had free raspberries in the back yard & I loved them. In the back yard & I ate them. & I ate them in the kitchen out of an aluminum pot. When I was thirty I loved raspberries, I loved to eat them. I loved the way they were made of many pieces in my mouth, & they came from the outside of the bush & the inside. They came from the outside in the sunshine & from the inside in the darkness, & that is where they went again. But inside in the darkness is where we are told the subconscious is & that is why I could not eat raspberries. I could not eat raspberries when I was three years old when we had free raspberries in the front yard. In Peachland, where the free raspberries grow, & they grew outside in the sunshine where I could reach them when I was three & a half. I could reach one & I ate it & I thought there was a bug on it. But I ate it too fast to know for certain. Years later I saw a face at a girl's window & I thought it was a man named Russell, but I went away too soon & so I never knew. I never knew whether I ate a bug on a raspberry. I had never eaten a bug before so I didn't know what they taste like. I could not eat raspberries for years after that day in our front yard when I was over three years old, even though the raspberries always look so good with all their round pieces in a cone or bunch. But there is a hole inside the raspberry & it could always have a bug in it.

CHAPTER 2: THE TEETER-TOTTER

Sometimes they are called see-saws, but that is in a school book or back east, & we always called them teeter-totters. Some had handles & others were plain boards, but for years I could not ride a teeter-totter. A very small child teeters before he rides, he is a tot. I was a tot in the darkness inside that is fear. I was afraid to ride the darkness because I was let down on the rocks. You must trust the boy on the other end, you must play the board. & he let me totter to the fall on the rocks. Because I fell I was afraid of that moment's darkness. The see-saw rises to the sun & drops to the darkness & the board is the same with a handle or without. I was inspired to be afraid of rising & I fell to the rocks. I cried that I could not trust the board but I could not trust the boy who let me rise & stept off the board to the rocks. My blood would rise in fear if I was near a teeter machine where I lost my blood to the rocks in falling. Up to the window, down to my elbow. Up to the top, down to the rocks. Up all my life, to down on the rocks. They were stones round tops out of the earth. I stood near the swings & teeter-totters at recess thinking of my school books, & what my fear is called in there.

CHAPTER 3: THE POLLYWOGS

Sometimes they are called tadpoles but that is in a school book or back east, & we always called them pollywogs. We always got them from the water under the railroad station. Somewhere it is called a bog but we always called it a slough. I loved to have them in a Mason jar with water from the tap, to watch them. You wanted to watch the legs come out but you never did. They were there one morning. You wanted to watch them when they were frogs but you never did. I cant remember why you never did. Not in jumping but in swimming.

Not in the grass but in the water. Not in the croaking but in the silent swimming with a tail. The tail would entirely disappear but I cant remember the tail disappearing. Almost, but not. It is a story someone was going to tell but I never heard it.

I heard the rocks on the hard dry earth baked & packt in our back alley. I walkt in the alley & saw the pollywogs where someone had overturned a jar of them & the water disappeared into the hot air or the baked earth. The pollywogs were a clump of jelly with no tails. They were silver in the sun. It was silver among the grey rocks on the earth.

CHAPTER 4: THE FLYING DREAM

The word from my hand follows the release of my eye
from the dream of my release from the ground but just.
Growing up is knowing all the evils of the world & failings
of all people

will not be corrected before the end of my life.

I was two & I was three & I was nearly four. I was one
with the ground, I was too good to be true, I was free of
the earth, I was for

correcting all the evils of the world & I would never die,
I would never begin dying. I flew standing up, maybe
six inches from the sidewalk. I could never get higher
but I could fly. I flew in the attitude of Jesus standing
on the water or above all on the mount of olives, Jesus
I thought I was. I began to think I was a superman or
Jesus because I could not be ordinary or what was the
use of being here inside my mind instead of out there
where they all were? In my dreams I never met anyone
flying toward me. I never grew all the way up, for later I
thought I was a poet, I had to be a poet or what was the
use of learning words & being inside my skull rather than
out there where they all are.

CHAPTER 5: THE BRUSH FIRE

I conceived my love for nature when I burned the hillside & this I did before I began school. The name of the town was Greenwood & when I returned a few years later the hill was green. I feared a spanking when I came home but received none & then I conceived my love for my parents.

The hillside burned, it burned faster than I could walk to step on the fire. Every step was on the blackened earth I was learning to love. I conceived my love for nature when I saw it burning faster than the men could get shovels into the earth.

The name of the town was Greenwood & the war was on, where cities burned in their cement. What held the hill together beneath the flames I did not know but I learned love for it & saw those men joined to the hill & my shame. That I could cause such peril while there was a war on.

I ran home & waited for the punishing hand while God allowed fire in the cities across the sea. It never came & when I went back a few years later the hill was covered with green wood while the nearby hills were brown & the war was over, & I loved it.

CHAPTER 6: THE VERANDAH

That house we lived in in Greenwood had a verandah wrapt in screen wire & a yard wrapt in white pickets taken from the old graveyard changing its fence for the old mining families who died during the turn of the century before the burning of the hill that glowed far later than the first smelter built at the turn of the century when Greenwood was the largest city between the prairie & the coast & died leaving the boast that it is now the smallest city in Canada because the mines are dead & the miners in the graveyard are long dead & the smelter is a dead fire with a dead chimney the highest structure in the area a spire I lookt up when I was five & when I was twenty & when I was thirty when I had raspberries in my back yard across Canada while the yard in Greenwood grew not berries but sweet peas that bloomed beside the white pickets so much depended on not now for the dead & nameless miners but my memory of the verandah I was allowed to sleep in summer nights in that quiet city so small & surrounded by green wood & close hills covered by holes dug by dead miners who named a nearby ghost town Deadwood where I always meant to go & never did though those fires have burnt ever since I heard the name spoken in that verandah shaded by the screen wrapt around.

CHAPTER 7: THE DEAR PATH

After I took it out I thought now I'm not the same, a girl's thought is my present thought. I found myself for the first time in the present. I find myself thinking about the death of the moth flopping around in front of me below the lamp where I write. That is slightly in the future & reading this will be further in the future but it will be the present. Now the moth is struggling on the floor & I will forget him till he flies here again.

I came back again & found the dear path of putting it in but I was already not the same & each time thereafter I was only by memory & the gift of the present not the same, a little.

I said to her how about running down & making me some eggs, so she did & brought them to me, she being older & a mother already & knowing I was proud & deciding to make me this present, not even thinking of the eggs we had exchanged but only of what she had said—you dont want to stop, do you? But I did not stop even then because the present continues not moving. I took her photograph & was careful with the f-stop, aiming the camera to catch the present forever. Now the photograph is a reminder of my past but I look forward every time for the present.

CHAPTER 8: THE BREAKS

Before I broke my nose the first time it turned up & I wisht it did not turn up & I got my wish. Before I broke my nose the second time it had a hump & I wisht it had no hump & I got my wish. Before I broke my nose the third time I was not reconciled to having a funny nose but I made no wish because I'd seen what that leads to twice but it broke again anyway. Before I broke my nose the fourth time I wisht I would break something else for a change & I got my wish. Before I broke the middle finger of my right hand I was working hard in the orchard & I wisht something would happen to me & I could quit working for a while & I got half of my wish. Before I broke my foot I wisht something would happen beyond my control to get my girl & I into bed together & I got a portion of my wish. Before I broke my hand I wisht I could impress my intended with the sincerity of my emotion & we got my wish.

Those are the breaks. We make our own breaks. We learn to take advantage of the breaks. We step on the breaks. We apply the breaks. The breaks even themselves up. We dont ask for more than our share of the breaks. Those are the breaks of the game.

CHAPTER 9: SOME DEATHS

My cousin Russell died the night before & I stayed on the lawn & said I didnt want his saxophone. It was a death without sex because he was twenty & I was twelve & we lived twenty-seven miles apart. In Penticton he played the saxophone & in Oliver I dreamed of playing the drums & that dream was dead & the duet was dead as well & after that I played alone but not the drums. They offered me the saxophone but I stayed by myself on the lawn.

My Aunt Dorothy died when I was a baby so I saw her but mainly in the photograph. She died of TB where she workt against death as a nurse. She workt against TB & she died & I never saw her photograph after I passt the age when she died & I had my chest photographt to see whether I had TB.

My grandmother Clara died at Easter & my grandfather Jabez walkt on his crutches around the living room saying "Mother" as if she would not be resurrected. He said it as if she were his mother, & he an old man. He said it as if she would not be resurrected & he a former minister of God. It was Easter & the food she had cookt for the family lay where she left it & began to undergo the changes brought by death. Perhaps it was thrown away & perhaps the family ate it all.

CHAPTER 10: THE SUBSTANCE

Inside the substance were the orange cheezies in the beaks of the mother duck & her ducklings swimming on the smooth pond. Inside the cheezies were the knobby knees of the gull standing in the still air on a round rock. Inside the rock was a rusty nail driven into a tree in the park. Hung on the nail was an inchworm hanging on the end of an unseen thread & the inchworm hung in front of my face in the sudden sunlight above a tap giving clear water that glistened in the sunlight. In the water was a flat fish glimmering all its colours on a flat rock drying in the continuous sunlight. Inside the fish was a thick tree trunk with a sworl of growth that told of its age begun before white men came to the coast. Inside the tree trunk was a white ice cream cone of soft ice cream that retained its conical shape going down my throat till the empty cone was left & became a part of the forest. Inside the empty cone was a high orange bridge that waved its narrow end back & forth as we walkt beneath its thick end on the edge of the rocky cliff. Across the bridge was a range of blue mountains I would never ascend high as I was here in the middle of the park.

CHAPTER 11: THE FRONT YARD

The song on the brown radio was pennies from heaven & I went to the front yard to look for the pennies or I imagined going to the front yard to look for pennies during the Depression where we had a hedge arching over the front gate & that was as close as I could get to heaven because I was three years old. I stood penniless in the Depression under the arch of hedge & watcht a square black car roll down the hill of our street toward the lake with no driver. I remember I saw there was no driver. Later I thought it was a trick; but my father could skip stones on the lake, he could skip a flat stone half way across the lake & later I found the lake was more than a mile across. I thought he had a power from heaven to skip stones like pennies across the lake, & while standing next to the clear water on flat stones I could see no square car in the lake. I thought the car had a power from heaven – I never imagined it was a runaway car. Though I wasn't know it was the Depression there were no runaway cars in the Depression. There is a picture of me wearing a large black hobo hat in the front yard. I am wearing it with no smile on my face & big round eyes. I am not carrying it upside down.

CHAPTER 12: THE DOOR

He swung the door behind him & fate was a swinging door. It was closing in front of my eyes on the porch & destiny is a door closing slowly. The door was coming to a close slowly. It was close to being shut slowly & there was a kitten standing. Chance is a kitten standing with its neck where a door was close to closing & I was watching sitting on the floor where my eyes were the curious eyes of the kosmos. H.G. Wells is able to teach that the kosmos is inscrutable & men with their eyes are curious. My I's were watching the slow door close on the kitten but the kitten was new so that slow was not slow & close was close enough & the kitten was strangling.

He came back & took the kitten to the garage & closed the door to me left without curiosity. I was left with guilt & guilt was silent. Guilt is not curiosity guilt is silent. He did not say anything when he came back from the garage. I thought he would have guilt but I had guilt & the guilt was like a closed door or it was like a kitten. I was curious about his guilt but I was filled with guilt about curiosity. I never knew till this minute how dangerous curiosity is.

CHAPTER 13: THE GUN

Malediction triggers euthanasia. The old poet put quietly to death by a gun full of bad words. His own the symptoms moving me to action. This happens over & over.

& is not over. Squeeze the trigger. Do not pull. Do not pull your punches but get it over as quickly as possible when it seems the kindest course.

Bad words flow from bad blood. In the Far East they are spilling good blood after bad, the blood of a young poet. What is he doing in there? Why does the old poet spill his bad words? Blood flows thru the young finger on the button in the far East.

The old poet holds the hand that signed the paper that repairs the house that Jack built. Jack was not killed with kindness, though the triggerman cited his bad words. He was felled when he came out of the woods into the city.

He was no longer in the East & he was no longer young. He was dead. Three little words are easier than three big words. The poet is dead short live the poet.

It is not really moving me to action. It is moving my action. It is in me. Like a bullet or a bad word.

CHAPTER 14: COMPOSITION

Consciousness is how it is composed. Consciousness is how it is composed. I told the Jungian professor there is no such thing as the subconscious, I decided to appear at his window where the blackness was & shout there is no subconscious. Consciousness is how it is composed. We cant go asleep I said & find out what we are thinking because then we are asleep. Or are we asleep. Consciousness is how it is composed. We are sometimes composed when we are awake. I think we are always being composed when we are awake & consciousness is how it is composed & we are it too because we are nobody's dream. When we dream we are awake. It is composed & not by us because we are in the composition. I say consciousness is how it is composed. Consciousness is how it is composed, & that is how we are conscious so we were never asleep composing. I wanted to appear at his window before he fell asleep & tell him I was no dream. I may be romantic but I am no dream. That is simply the way I am composed. I am composed by him & composed by me & they are different but they are not dreams they are consciousness. That is how they are different & that is composition.

CHAPTER 15: GROWING

In grade six I was interested in science but before I knew the pleasure of its order then it was only a gleam. In grade nine I was interested in science fiction for the pleasure of it was only a dream not the order intended but all along I was practising a pleasure in order but that was superstition & certainly not science fiction. In grade twelve after the order of six & nine I was interested in fiction & seeking an order that would be clean knowing superstitiously that fiction was certainly not the novel it was certainly not news it was moulding that is not science but something like movement where you do not concern yourself with what you are riding but with the present of where you are not going but you are right now, moving. Science wants to know where you have been & where it will take you. That is order & may even be orders though that sounds like romance. Romance is not certainly fiction though it may be science fiction. In grade three I was interested in my dog & his associations with the animals in the orchard. I lived in a house surrounded by trees in efficient lines so that the house was connected with highway 3 & 97 by a straight gravel driveway & at the end of the driveway was a garage behind which I grew wheat in hopes of feeding the chickens.

CHAPTER 16: PLACE OF BIRTH

My mother sat in the lawyer's office to swear I was born. She sat there thinner than the last minute I was borne in her belly. The lawyer was suborned to complete the story of my birth. The story of my birth is on paper hidden somewhere in a truthful mother's room. I say he was suborned because the question was a lie & still is, for those who will not open their eyes. I say I was born & where. Since then I have decided to say where it was I was born many times in different places. My mother sat in the office & swore I was born in the first place in the same time. Since then I have sworn to decide I was born when it was at many different times. My mother was the contributor & the notes on contributors are suborned to swear just where & when & they are sworn to secrecy. Composition is not there it is going to be there & you are here & that is where & you might believe when. My mother sat composed in her chair & told the story of my birth & where. Consciousness is how it is composed & starts with birth or some say earlier. I began to be composed at such & such a time in such & such a place. Science wants to know where you have been & where it will take you & so does the Canada Council. I tell them what my mother said in her chair & when & where.

CHAPTER 17: THE CODE

I crackt the Captain Marvel code without paying to join the club & that has something to do with it. It is having something to be doing with it. Not necessarily to be being more clever than XZKGZRM NZIEVO but more than the ones who are joining & paying & not thinking about the importance of the & a. It is not so much composing as the imposing & breaking the code to break the imposing. The letters are impostors easily broken & composing is not there it is going.

To be there but we are here, on this side of the page begging to be seen breaking. The code broken is no breaking of the law it is the discovering of the law. The law is covered by a code begging to be crackt. Moses & the making of Captain Marvel that big red cheese both to be broken on the alphabet doubled on itself. I was still mosaic when I broke the puzzle & put it together with the help of the & a.

The code is broken article by article & that is the gradual making of the making of the law. That is the marvel to be seeing what they who are joining & paying are not seeing that is the making of the law uncovered.

CHAPTER 18: THE TREES

I pickt in the orchard removing cherries. I moved in the orchard thinning apples dropping them like soldiers on the grass. I passt thru the orchard packing pipes for sprinkling thru the grass full of wet slugs. I walkt thru the orchard piping songs of joy & saw what I never had seen. I sang in the orchard plucking apricots & thoughts of Doukhobor girls obscene but innocent as I stood on the ladder plucking. Prunes & plums & peaches & pears. I stood later picking apples into a bag strapt to my body & thought of Polly the girl on the ladder. I passt thru the orchard pulling suckers from the trunks of the trees. I drove a tractor thru the orchard dragging a trailor covered with props for the heavy branches of the trees. I pulled a trailor piled with boxes & I piled heavy boxes behind the trailor & the piles of boxes under the trees were homes for mice & wet slugs. Guilt is not curiosity guilt is silent. I never told the girls under the poison trees. I never sprayed the trees in the spring that was another's job I would not do & they would not ask me. I stood on the highest branches in the orchard & worried about the flight of my soul. I stood on the ladder plucking. I sat on the boxes smoking. I lay on the grass eating sandwiches. I walkt home from the orchard with its dust on my boots & green or red stains on my fingers.

CHAPTER 19: WORKING & WEARING

I discovered the working was a wearing away. In the orchard at Naramata I removed my baseball cap every time & every time it was a nest of hair & I was fifteen there. The working was a wearing away. On Sundays I wore the cap at baseball & lost no hair & Sunday was the best day there. Who bets on Sunday lets his hair grow. The machine that works is worn away & oiled every day. When I was fifteen I oiled my hair & made a nest I was wearing there.

In the forest near Merritt I carried two cloves in my jaw for the holes of pain I carried there. There was no dentist working where I carried my pain from forest to town. I used to drown the cloves in beer in the parlours there. I wore the cloves in the widening holes & on Sundays at baseball I knew no pain save the times I would err & never be forgiven. The working was the time of wearing away.

The sun is dying to keep us alive. The fire in its place is dying to keep us warm. What is working is being worn.

CHAPTER 20: THE BREAKS

I broke my nose on a girl's heel. I broke my foot under a ladder. I broke my nose on a baseball. I broke my finger under a wagon. I broke my nose on a man's fist. I broke my hand against a concrete wall. I wisht my nose did not turn up & I broke it. Has the cat got your tongue? I wish my nose did not have a hump in it & I broke it. Who told you to hold your tongue? I wisht my nose was not pusht to one side & I broke it & it was pusht over to the side. Investigate him. Seek the vestiges of his movement. Look for footprints. Gumshoe investigator, break the case.

He wants to know why the bones are broken & why they are not stronger where they broke him. He calls a strike on you if you break your wrists. I broke my nose again on a baseball. I struck the wall behind burlap & broke my fist.

Birney broke his fast thru a wired-shut jaw. Jerry broke across the street & a car hit him now he's in traction. Lionel was hit by a car that left him broken on the street. The wagon was free from the tractor & it broke my finger. Jesus Christ, I said. They broke the back of my car on the wet dark street.

I got too close & the foot broke my nose. It was the first. It was right in front of my brain.

CHAPTER 21: COME

I tasted my sperm on my finger. I had come full circle. I remembered Willy saying George what is this white stuff. The first time the smell is fresh, after that you don't notice. It did not taste as it smelled but that was later. That was later in the circle. The testes are drawn as circles & then the weight makes them hang & they are ovals. It was worth the wait. Worth their weight in gold she said tasting it. It doesnt taste so bad as you'd think. What would you think. It beats meeting a monster who has circled behind you. Put it all behind you it was worse the waiting than when it came.

The coming was all of a sudden he said it just came. Later he said I came but that was later after the second coming. It is the same white stuff. Is it dangerous? No, I tasted my coming on my finger. She came round to that too, full circle. I made her full & she came & later I tasted her coming on my finger. That was the second coming. When you get older you'll come only once she said or you wont come round at all.

Why given round heads if not for eternity I said. Taste my tongue in your ear she said.

CHAPTER 22: THE BACK YARD

Back in the yard in Greenwood where the pickets of the fence were from the graveyard a deer hung from a wire & it was dead. In the back yard in Greenwood the chicken lost his head & flew to the roof crowing blood from his white neck turning red. From the roof in Greenwood my father threw water on the dogs where their necks were red with bites to the bone. The deer was brought home. The chickens lived in a shed. The dogs are dead.

The chicken was on the kitchen table where my mother tore its colours from its hole & they were yellow & purple they were clean & circles tumbling over circles. The deer was hung till the blood would flow going to his head. He was bigger than I the chicken was smaller than I the dog my size with my eye on him seeing that he did not leave the back yard in Greenwood for a fight.

I later burned the mountain down where the plants perisht for a while. Did I eat the deer. I did not eat the chicken. I ate the eggs & watcht the kittens being born behind the stove in the kitchen. In the back yard my sister was chased into the kitchen by a rooster. We had written bad words about her on the shed. Later I visited & the dog was dead. Later I visited & the mountain was green & it was not a mountain.

CHAPTER 23: IT HAPPENED

What I knew about that nobody knew about was the private delight taking a part in erosion. Start the small pebble rolling down the mountain. The delight. I believed it was possible all men share a brain but nobody gave a sign they would know about this. Would anyone understand taking an inch of bark off the pine tree bark. Saving nickels in a jar. Taking part in erosion & it is not doing what nature would not have done if I wasnt there in it. It was doing what nature did while I was there in it. The pure delight of cutting your fingernails of filling the waste basket. Of watching the speedometer turn to 70,000 of taking your eyes off the road to watch the disappearance of the nines. Taking a part in erosion. Hating Christmas but buying a present when a cheque for poetry comes in.

I burned a log in the fire. I buried a baseball in the earth. I broke a test tube. I put an axe thru my caulkt boot. I lost a tooth in the masht potatoes. I burned down a hillside. I grew wheat beside the garage. I peeled the cucumbers. I rolled a boulder over a cliff. I cut the rattles off a snake with my six iron. That was delight. It didnt happen because I was there. I was where it happened & it happened & I knew someone must know but I wondered.

CHAPTER 24: THE FRUIT RANCH

It was sweet. It was sweet & sometimes cold. If the ruts in the road were frozen. It was sweet if it was biting into the apple. Delicious. A little frozen at the core. Not ice but a little frozen yesterday morning at the core. It was sweet if it was warm. For instance the sun shining on the puppy's golden belly & you put it against your face & smell it the sun moving a little & eyes that are not frightened. My uncle visited all his trees gathering fruit for the wine in the kitchen. The ruts in the road were seldom frozen. When they were we walkt on the white ice this morning in the puddles & they crackt at step by step. The sun hammered into the sky. Can you see that? Sweet sweet sun & ice that is white under foot. When the ruts are not frozen the mud is scraped off at the door of the kitchen or it is caught in balls between the puppy's toes for he is older now. My uncle was not embarrasst by his rubber country boots standing at the door to the kitchen. When the ruts in the road are not muddy the dust is a foot deep. I drive the tractor & raise dust around my naked chest where I turn to look at the trailor & burn my shoulder with the new cigarette. I wear my baseball cap black with a white N on the front. That is sweet & so I am not embarrasst.

CHAPTER 25: ROGER FALLING

He had only recently learned to walk but he was falling on his head just outside the back porch where the kitten was choked that was not there now neither kitten nor back porch. The porch was ript away & there were planks making a ramp & beside them an excavation with concrete walls & the bottom covered with round boulders because Lawrence or Oliver is in the path of an old late ice age glacier. He was falling or pusht by a deliveryman into the excavation this was my little brother Roger nine years younger than I was he was falling head first into the path of the glacier on his head nine feet down on a boulder. My brother, I had first heard of him outside the back porch doing my back yard duties, how do you like having a little brother my father said. It wasnt guilt till I thought they might think it guilt I watcht it but not like the cat I went, it was just slow or panic, into the kitchen hollering Roger's in the excavation & my sister tried to pick him up & carry him up & out. How do you like having a little brother, he could just barely walk & now he slept in the dark room near the elm trees with me with a steel clamp in his skull with a plaster bandage around his head, how do you like your new hat, we called it Roger's new hat but that night he was asleep & I prayed in the room that God would let him live & let his skull be all right. I dont remember him falling. All right.

CHAPTER 26: THE CHILDHOOD

She was always asking did you have a happy childhood & I was always saying a happy childhood I dont know or I suppose so I dont know. Well she would say would you say you had an unhappy childhood. I dont know I would say an unhappy childhood I guess I would say I had an unhappy childhood but only for a reason & then it wouldnt be an unhappy childhood I suppose you would say. She would say as she was always saying then what kind of childhood was it really. I would always say I dont know what kind of childhood was it really I suppose sometimes it was happy & sometimes I was unhappy but it was not unhappy it was that I was unhappy but not it because even when I was unhappy it was in all probability happy. She would always be saying then I simply ask you was it or is it a generally happy childhood or a generally unhappy childhood. I guess it was all in the way you look at it for a reason I would say thinking of her childhood. She wanted to have me ask about her childhood was it generally a happy childhood or generally an unhappy childhood but I would say it depends on the reason you would want to say whether it was a happy childhood or not.

CHAPTER 27: ST. LOUIS

I was playing cards when the long distance phone call came to tell me they would publish my novel. Was I excited? Of course, I was winning. About the novel? Oh but I had already had books of poems publisht, I already had books. Was I excited about them. We had almost publisht a book by Tishbooks in 1963. Was I excited doing that. I had seen my poems publisht in magazines in Eastern Canada & Central Canada, all of which we called Eastern Canada as they do in football & the air cadets. Was that a thrill. I was a failure in air cadets. The poems in eastern magazines. I had got paid for my first poem in a magazine right there in Vancouver. Was it exciting to see it printed & to get paid for it. Not much pay. To get paid though. But the poem had already been publisht in the university magazine & the illustration & design were better there. Was that quite exciting. I had already publisht poems & prose in the magazine in earlier issues. Was I excited the first time. I was used to it because before that I saw my writing every week in the air force newspaper. Was that a kick. In high school my stories were in the annual every year. Was that a nice part of being in school. I was more interested in the weekly baseball & basketball stories I sold by the inch to the out-of-town paper. A good feeling for a kid to see his words in the paper then. I had been selling my baseball & basketball stories to the local paper for years. I wanted to be a sports writer for the *St. Louis Post-Dispatch*.

CHAPTER 28: THE LAKE

In the water was a flat fish glimmering all its colours but mainly yellow perch eating its brother on the end of the line. I yankt him out & we cut him up & who was with me was I think Fred whom I thought of today nearly forty but then I thought of him hanging from the trestle by his fingers at that same lake saying to his girlfriend Barbara she'd better call him pet names or he would let go & drop to the rocks & she did. Before that she was my girlfriend & he was an older kid from Belgium. We cut up the yellow perch & used him for bait & I never caught another fish but I killed a pregnant squirrel with a stone thrown into the high fir tree & I killed a snake on the golf course with my six iron & sent the six rattles to Amanda or Angela the lady anyway on Vancouver Island, I sent them in an envelope & she called me Saint George & soon Saint George was removed from the list of saints. Fred & I made a raft & sailed it on the lake reputed to have no bottom though we never went in our lives to the north end where there was a house lived in by six nuns. It was called Gallagher Lake & was near Gallagher Bluff & I have never found out who Gallagher was but Barbara was Gregory, a saint still on the list.

CHAPTER 29: THE FIRST TWO TOWNS

What is a town, what is a town exactly that we have lived in or a city, what is the city that we have lived in even less or a good deal more depending on how we look at it. How do we look at it & how did we look at it. Well in the first place it was mainly towns & in the second place it was nearly all cities & you should say time as well as place for town or city.

The first was Penticton. It was Penticton & I was born on the hill but I did not look at Penticton from the hill & now when I am in Penticton though now I am not in Penticton I look up at the hill but I did not look down from the hill because I was just born there where my father climbed to see me & now I am realizing that he is old & if he hears this I love him.

The second was Peachland though it was really the first for I because that was where I began to look at a town though really I began to look at the lake or across the lake to the east side because I was fated to be in the west looking east in these imaginings because I would always move eastward looking backward to the west not really looking east but being there.

CHAPTER 30: THE THIRD TOWN

From Peach land to Green wood to Greenwood where I learned love & burned the hillside & it was green & far past the hill because I was little though didnt realize it was Deadwood, a place I never visited with real eyes. I had real eyes in Greenwood where there was white snow. White white white, white snow. White snow. I learned to run down the hill on my sleigh over seedlings poking their way green above the white snow & my green blade before me would slay the shoots & my blood was red on the white snow. The blood of the white chickens was red on the white snow & red on the white chickens. The blood of my dog Caesar the second was red on the white dog. The deer hung by his feet & his blood was red between the hairs on his side. My mother spoke often of a side of beef. Bad words flow from bad blood. We spoke of the Japanese who had twins & sacrificed one of them on a stone cairn that came from the bloody picture in my family's Bible. The Japanese wore black clothes in the white snow. It was war time & we had blackouts & the moon shone on the white snow. The pickets of the fence were from the graveyard. But the Japanese burned their bodies & melted a circle in the white snow. White white white white, white. The egg on the bench began white & weeks later it was dark & that chicken never scratcht in the white snow.

CHAPTER 31: THE FOURTH TOWN

It is really a village. It is still a village. I was embarrasst that Oliver or Lawrence was only a village & I waited for them to vote & pay their taxes & become with pride a town or later with great pride a city. I could hardly wait to live in a city. It is however really a village. There were two populations, one thousand & five thousand, but four thousand lived outside the village in the orchards, but I always said five thousand. Consciousness is how it is composed. When they askt I said I was from Penticton, this was when I was back east & Penticton got famous for the hockey champions. There was no hockey in the village of Oliver & that is why it was always a village. At first we lived in an absent soldier's house in an orchard two miles from the village & he later became Conservative member of parliament to my shame. Secondly we lived in an orchard less than two miles from the village but off a back road not the highway now. Then we moved to the village & I had more pride but the house was small & covered with tar paper & the owner lived next door on the corner lot. We made the house larger & I became friends with people who lived in the village & gave up my friends who lived in the orchards. Later I went to work for people who owned the orchards & they were strangers & my bosses.

CHAPTER 32: THE FIRST CITY

It was certainly pleasant being there in Victoria. It was certainly not too big to be first & certainly not too small either to be a city, the first. It was certainly pleasant & odd to live on an island & to tell yourself you are living on an island & in a city & at university away from home. But it was not really away from home & it was certainly pleasant there because she was there too who had lived three miles outside the village & it was certainly true that you went to that university because she was there though perhaps certainly perhaps because your uncle Jack lived a few blocks from the university on Henderson there in Victoria.

It was certainly pleasant though odd to come from a village with a man's name because of a premier to a city with a woman's name because of a queen. She certainly has her name all over the world & here in this city & on this university & certainly in the future on many things here many years after her death though she was a queen. She had nothing to do with it. It was certainly pleasant for reasons & the reasons were never to do with a queen. She was certainly no queen though she once lived in Britain & later in the village or three miles down the road or highway in an area named for a hamlet that never materialized called Testalinda.

CHAPTER 33: THE EXTRACTIONS

The code is broken article by article, as teeth are, as confidence is, & once it was triumphant to break the mystery but now it is sad because one loses confidence. They put it in my arm & in my jaw & they put it in my lungs so it would get into my brain & probably my heart & I did go to sleep, yes fully to sleep. I woke with the pain or pressure an insistent one-note music & I heard them, the dentist & his woman or women, though I was not fully awake, it was the first intimation that I was going to break the code. He was a fraud, using old they must have been air force or Osoyoos expressions & I struggled to awaken & get out of the chair & the drug, they had drugged me & I was at their mercy. The woman said no & held me down & he was pulling the last tooth, he was supposed to be a surgeon but he was a fraud, making money. I have never been able to forget that. The insistent one chord droned loudly as in my childhood crazy fear when I could not break the code to explain to my mother who said no what is it, angrily, there is nothing there. But now I can have no confidence in doctors just when I need it because I am not a child now, I am getting older now with rotten teeth. They had drugged me & I was at their mercy, certainly at their mercy. We are at their mercy & it is sad to wake up afraid & angry out of the drug with them holding us down & using old air force expressions for a tough job when they think we are asleep.

CHAPTER 34: THE ACTS

Things. Events & things. I have found this out about events & things. I have found this out that events & things cannot act upon. You cannot be acted upon by events & things & you could not in the past. Each time thereafter you are only by memory & the gift of the present not the same, a little. You are not the same & that is actual. It is not factual, & it is not real. It is actual. There are events & there are things but they are not actual until you are there to act. You are an actor & they are not & they may not act upon you. *Agir, agir,* that is the verb of the person & not the event or the thing. You are an event & a thing living as a person when you act upon. Existentialism is a conspiracy of the mind tempted by discourse & its electrical child the radio. The radio cannot turn you off & on. *Agir* is not a verb of the radio. You cannot be acted upon by the radio or by events on the radio. You can arrive, lift it, & act & act upon. You are a thing or an event until you act but that is not true or actual, it may be real but it is not actual. Man is: he does. The thing does not do, it is. Done to. Done to is not event, it is act. Man is not except as he does. Before that he is only real & that is not enough. The baby acts before he knows about real, before he steps into the river that is a thing during an event, acted upon.

CHAPTER 35: THE NEXT PLACE

The next place is really a series of places so that the next place is really time, that is, a series, not as on the railroad, though that is certainly, there, but I was in the force, & we always had a town or city nearby, & though we thought we thought it was always different we always acted as if it was the same, perhaps, because we were, where we were, was always the same, though we spoke always of the difference, from time to time, of the place, & so, there you are. The next place, then, is always, a series of times, & we were always careful about time, & here I am, speaking of "we," so there we are. Going into the town or city, St. Jean, & Barrie, & Portage, & always the certainty of what they drank there, & the certainty of girls, which was never a certainty, but it was supposed to be, & we, supposed. What was factual & what was real, what was actual. I can, not, deny now that time is converted into space, or we subsumed one into the other. The next place is really, a series of what they drank, & what they danced, & we were waiting, always, for the time. For a vulgar instance, the pubs in Portage closed the bar at nine forty-five & we arrived at the dance at ten fifteen & the taxi cost fifty cents, & what of the next place. In the force there was rank, & we filed for time.

CHAPTER 36: THE POOL

It was the empty pool & then it was the cool hospital. It was ninety-nine in the shade & then in the hospital I was laid in white sheets. There was no shade & I was not afraid I was too stupid with the sun to be afraid. I was struck with the sun & in love with my luck & I thought I was the sun of god. Simply, I was in the hospital with sunstroke. My temperature was far above ninety-nine but I was in the catholic hospital of sheets as white as the sun & my grandfather's hair. That would have made him the father of god but he was a retired preacher.

My job was to clean the algae from the empty pool made of concrete in the hot sun. The blinding sun turned white & I awoke to the sheets next to my eyes sore with sunstroke. Later I always needed glasses but didnt have them. I squinted.

The sun god saw to it with his eye. Simply, I was in the hospital half blind with algae in my eyes. Sun stroke brings on too hard a headache for metaphor, simply makes you squint. My twin eyes began to bend in different directions, son of man & struck by sun, struck like a new coin, mint in the middle of the concrete.

CHAPTER 37: FAINTING

Today the beautiful woman has a black eye from fainting & falling on the floor & we spoke of fainting. The first time I fainted & other times. The lovable man said talk in there about the pain. Can I do both. No, I cannot do both & I am more drawn to talk about fainting & being knockt out. In the comics or funnies as our country friends & aunties called them they faint or are knockt out with a bird in a balloon & crosses for eyes & smiles with closed mouths. The first time I was knockt out. I misst the soccer ball & fell down to the rocks. They were round stones out of the ground where we had a glacier. Ice on the forehead wakes up the fainted girl. I had no ice but I awoke with four carrying me into the school that was the old scout hall where we went during wartime crowding & no wood for building. Up all my life, to down on the rocks. I was proud & yes I did see stars, they have stars as they have stars in the comics but no bird & certainly the stars did not stand still as they had to in the comics. I had always thought they would stand still & be larger & not so bright but many colours. That was in 1944 & in 1957 I fainted with no stars but large grey masses that were perhaps the code & I fainted really fainted into a chair & the grey masses continued in my belly where they would remove a useless organ. In the photograph of the group I am the only one without a smile with closed mouth an hour before I fainted & I cant remember the pain. That is the reason for fainting.

CHAPTER 38: THE CLOVES

Cloves are a spice & a flavour for a lifesaver & cloves are stuck in pigs when theyre dead. I had cloves in the two holes in my teeth all day walking thru the bush near Merritt where there was no dentist & this was all summer, 1958, great pain & broken shoes. There was no dentist & I was afraid of him & the future when he would be there the dentist. I walkt thru the forest & I forget my shoes but they stept on broken ground & the pain came up my bones to my teeth where the cloves were. It doesnt taste so bad as you'd think. What would you think. That I was Jesus & could fly out of here with my cloves. Out of the forest, up to the birds that I spoke to with my pain, my shirt pocket filled with cloves for the long days & during the nights I drank beer & the beer was flavoured with clove going thru my teeth. There was no dentist & I learned not to be afraid of the pain on the days it would come I nearly learned to love it. All day walking thru the bush with fifty pounds of paint on my back in a can yellow or sometimes blue, the colour of no lifesaver. I knew by then I was not Jesus. I knew by Jesus I could not fly, I had to walk weighing fifty more pounds & I pounded my feet in their boots bouncing pain up the bones to my broken teeth where the cloves were.

CHAPTER 39: THE FINGERS

It wasnt my fault, he said she could get his briefcase from the car on the pebbles & I ran for the car, it was grey as the pebbles, maybe to beat her maybe to make her hurry as in a game & she slammed the door of the car on her hand & cut the end of her little finger, off. It hung from a piece of skin & they were disgusted with me I thought before they drove away out the pebble driveway to Dr. Bridgeman who sewed it back on & there was that much anyway. It was not my fault. Dr. Bridgeman delivered her first baby where she suffered, my sister, that had nothing to do with me.

This wasnt my fault either, she was my first girlfriend but I would lose her to my friend Fred who was there at the time, then, I was holding the paring knife making really a game of it but she reacht for it & I pulled it away, toward me, it was a natural instinct, I didnt want her to touch it. The end of her little finger hung by a piece of skin & I was given to understand I wasnt coming with them to the doctor downtown when he would sew it back, on. I'm not sure whether he was Dr. Bridgeman, but it wasnt my fault & that is when I began really to understand that she was Fred's girlfriend, in all likelihood his first. There is by way of contrast the pure delight of cutting your fingernails. There will be a time & when it is time they are ready to come off. There is no blame & no pain & there never was.

CHAPTER 40: THE JOINTS

I could work in cold storage because of the heat. The heat filled the peaches with juice & my hands afterward, especially on Sunday when I did not put on my old winter air force clothes & go into the refrigerated room out of the room into the railroad car into the hot sun, the fingers curled around wooden handles of the hand truck, curled till I could not open them like blossoms of the peach trees. I feel it now in the back of my right hand, the tree of arthritis, I could not sleep those nights without my mother's pills, waking in the morning with my hands curled till I'd spilled the coffee, yes it's working now, out in the sun & again at lunch. The doctor, I forget his name save that he was not Dr. Bridgeman, told me it was not crippling but it was arthritis & I was proud to have it, age twenty-one.

When it rains, yes, when it rains, just like they say in some pained humour they seem to need, when it rains, the tree grows & shoots like arteries all thru, like they say, arthritic smile, it's the pain, totally private, it's mine, & I have it & am still, I admit it, glad to have it, but later I will not & will try not to have it, the numbing & wonderful private pain totally inside.

CHAPTER 41: THE CLAMPS

I was going to get my chance to play ball twice, the first time I was just drying the dishes for my mother on the weekend before the game in Oliver & I dropt the mixmaster bowl into the sink & caught it on the short hop just as it broke cutting my hand next to the main nerve the doctor said, I think it was Dr. White, surely the bowl was white as no ball we ever played with then was white. It was white & the sink was white white white, white while I closed my eyes & when I opened my eyes it was red, red on white, red on the white chicken, red again. We drove down to see Dr. White on his weekend & he put steel clamps in. I can still see the scar & the little light points where the clamps went in. The pliers put them in neatly & later spread them neatly & pulled them out.

In Abbotsford I was catcher for the B.C. team & we were in the playoffs & the night before the game I broke my nose playing baseball in the dusk. They wanted to take me to the hospital in Vancouver & I said no & next day I blinkt trying to catch & played left field instead, where I made a great catch going away & blood filled my nose where I could not see the colour. Jacques Laperrière played six games with a broken wrist & they didnt want the press to know. He said so tonight after they won the cup. We won & I wonder whether the others remember. This is more plain & then again it is not.

CHAPTER 42: THE DOGS

I have dogs but do I seem to have dogs always. I am wondering & not now but often. I am wondering whether I love my dogs or even like them. Not just sometimes but in general. Are they splendid. Would I suffer if they disappeared or died. The first dog I or we had was Caesar & I dont remember what happened to him. That was I believe in Peachland but maybe to some extent in Greenwood. In Greenwood there was a cat who had kittens behind the stove & also Caesar the second dog named that & he was definitely my dog because they brought him to my bed Christmas Eve & he scratcht me. He was a wire-haired terrier & he bit Uncle Red's wire-haired terrier named Beans, I just now remembered, to the bone. In the orchard near Oliver we tied him to an apple tree & drove to Summerland & when we came back he was gone. It is not doing what nature would not have done if I wasnt there in it. There was soon afterward Monty the golden cocker & when we moved into the village we gave him to Uncle Gerry so he could go on living in an orchard away from traffic & there he was run over by a tractor in the orchard. Later there was Dinky the old dog with the S-shaped burn on her back who came back with me in the car from Greenwood where my Grandfather Emmet or his wife had just died & I just now remember they were living in our old house there.

CHAPTER 43: THE FLESH

Nobility, nobility, hate the word but do it, hate the words but live off them, hate the words as Hemingway taught but do the deed as Hemingway taught who was called Ernest. She had an abortion & I was not the father. She had it & I thought I was not the father. I thought I could not be the father. I think now I may have could have been the father but I couldnt have though I love it. Her father thought I was the father or I thought so. Nobility, hate the thought but the deed is father to the thought & that was before linguistics or was it. Who was father & who cares because there was no child though when I met her I or rather she should have been a child, she was seventeen. In the tennis court, on the bed. Dresst in long skirts, housed in her own suite in the house. It was likely there & it was there that I let it be known or thought by her father or likely others. Not for pride, not that sort of pride in any case. He said it just came, it just read off the page. Write a novel unlike Hemingway save for the author, hating nobility but ensuring that they see the deed. The deed was outside the house, not in. Her father paid for it & someone else did it & I remained silent. No one ever called me a savage.

CHAPTER 44: THE SPIDERS

When I got there I sat in the car unnoticed & lookt at my bald fat friend knocking spiders off the flowers with a broom. My sister had a black widow from the basement in a Mason jar & she fed it the insects that came into the house. I was bitten on the eyelid by a spider, there are no non-poisonous spiders. This which is not so strange is the more used & it walks on its own number of legs & it goes there, there is the writing. When I got there it was not but when I was there it began to get there, it has managed to get there, especially when we do not manage. We composed ourselves in the living room & my friend sat there most of him unnoticed while I tried to knock down the webs in front of him, it was not sad then but it is so sad. In this house there are some insects but in that house there are none & I think of writing a poem for Monica, she is the daughter, her voice like a spider, not the voice of a spider, like a spider. When I got there I sat in the car unnoticed & lookt at the house with all its curtains drawn where no insect could enter. Simply he is my old bald fat friend & she is inside the house where no light comes in the window & Monica counts the countries on the map. It is going to be there & you are here. You sit unnoticed in the car & look out the window. The car has eight windows.

CHAPTER 45: THE OPERATIONS

So pleasing is disaster, I want you to hold still while I tell you the stories of my operations. So easy is the laughter now, they say it'll keep you in stitches but it would not. It would not but that is long enough ago, yes, so ancient is being old enough in the matter. Even the water we see from our beach here gusht from his side & it is too late to tell that story, hold still. You bastard you bastard I said to my own body, part of my body I want you to hear about. It is my body & it rimes, this is the basis for composition & autobiology it is going to be there if you can hold still long enough for it. Hold still he said this is going to hurt & the water gusht out & a wave will cover the toes of your shoes if you stand still. So pleasing is disaster when you are old enough & it is old enough it is right there, right there, in front of you, like a wave that has stood still. Operation in my throat operation in my belly operation on my hand operation in my mouth hold the line please. It does not shatter, it usually does not shatter, it cuts & folds back softly & the water comes out mixt with blood, red again, the whiteness of a powder dissolved & sent into, it is nice to be this old, between operations. The body of the work gets tired as the body gets tired & that is your own biology & it is not disaster, it may need an operation. Foot by foot, tonsils, appendix, hand, & jawbone.

CHAPTER 46: IT

It was not a loud buzzing but it was like a loud buzzing & my mother came into the room & said what is it & what was it, a private thing to be afraid of & possess & I couldnt tell her & she was angry at me the same old son, George uncontrollable. It was not just a loud buzzing but also not the right distances, the things in the room were too far away & not coming closer & in the daytime I connected it with the double vision, two of everything you could live with. It wasnt madness because I was inside it. No it was not sad, it was true. It was not a loud constant buzzing or humming but it was what would be there besides the sound if there was a loud buzzing or humming. It was there. It was there & they were outside it, they could not hear it but I could not hear it but it was different & so was I. If I stared at the things they did not go away but they were too far as if I were looking from high in an airplane but the things were of a scale to appear as if the airplane were on the ground but the airplane was high in the air but it had nothing to do with airplanes. I still do not know what it was but it was not a loud buzzing. My mother said what & I just knew or said it it it it it it it & it was all around but she was not in it & she could not hear it but it was not a thing to hear or be in, it was there.

CHAPTER 47: THE SCARS

I received the scars & I was proud of them. I received the scars & increast the stories in order to be proud of them. Something sharp in the quicksand left a scar on my shin but now was it quicksand. I have always wondered was it quicksand though I went down. A scar on my shin, grade three, let it go that's what I'm doing. I let go or did I let go I've always said I jumpt off the forbidden outhouse roof into my father's hands or did I let go. Triangular scar near my armpit I see every six years. Any distinguishing marks. I received the scars & I was able to make myself proud of them because the circumstances were forbidden, is that what it was. No, I have discusst what it was or rather what it was not & it was not quite the forbidden. Some people take this easy, retiring to their rooms & writing. Scar on my cock or is it really a natural line after all this time or did I receive it with no drug, my father & the doctor in Summerland holding me down while he did the cutting. Probably around but I have thought always till recently lengthwise, another story I may have increast. If my skin is to be cut I will possess the marks. Scar under my eyebrow from Jerry's head under the basket. Scars at the base of both thumbs. Scar across my belly. Scar under the hair becoming visible on my scalp. How hard is it to be increasing the distinguishing marks as we near the ending of this.

CHAPTER 48: THE BODY

The body is not muddy it is hardly muddy it is muscles yes it is still muscles with less hair at the knee & calf where it has worn pants. The body is not muddy it has worn places especially the knee & calf where the hair was & is almost gone & there is no hair where the scars are. There are also parts where the eye can never see & they are not worn by the eye behind glass & they are worn nevertheless. I am sometimes weary of having worn the body for so long but I will not say that, goodbye to all that, so long. So long hair it has been so long, it has never been so long but it is worn. It was sweet & sometimes cold. The body is not now nor has ever been muddy, that is clear. I am in the middle of a stream & my body is the stream & what is the boat. The body is not muddy it is mostly water & so was my mother, she was the first stream the primal stream I floated out on to the land I landed on making a bit of mud with my water. There are parts the eye cannot see because they are in the past they tell us has done just that, what a view of the stream. If this is the stream & I am still to float what is the boat. What is the boat.

At War with the U.S.

Vancouver
January 11, 1973–August 15, 1973

(Talonbooks, 1974)

1

There comes a time
when we must
take measures

2

I pulled the carbon paper from between the pages

The white page said page five
The yellow page said page six

I have never written anything that fast

Especially this
slow slow
page one

3

The instant I saw
the young bearded man
swing by with crutches & one leg

I thought: he's been in Viet Nam

So that's what passes
thru minds in the USA
every day

Yes American life
is transparent

Hi Mom, hi Dad, hi Son
take it easy sitting down in California

4

1945
I said when the war is over
there wont be any more newspapers

Wise kid
nine years old

I had been afraid of that
since 1942

I still love the paper
when I buy it

& when I finish it there wasnt much
but another one tomorrow

5

I saw it
from the train window
from the television helicopter

the dark, dark, stony forest
where pleistocene eyes watch
the sky turn fishy, turn black

& no foot falls
shod

But we trim nickel, we tame electrons
we buzz the land. Our buttons
break on the soil of Yankee-torn Cambodia

300 years & a few miles from stone age
to splintered atoms, how have we
hurt our fresh-cut home so fast

6

& who are we

The sheer
intensity
& numbers of their bombs—

they are trying to obliterate
measure, the inevitable measure

& making count of themselves

We help them count
one two three

They see their fear
walking out of the bush
four five six

7

I write as they
walk by my window—

how quickly, a half-
sentence & they are gone

girding themselves at the general store
for the war of words

8

Let's do something
we've always done
for a change

9

Reader I just want you here right now

Later you may go where you will

I just want to get the counting over with

the exchange of prisoners

to detach a name from nature's hodge podge

This is my moment, our moment

10

The white car
below my window
has a window
in which I see
my daughter's
one year old head

She is off to her war called school

I wave
& my fingers look like hers
save that they hold
a pen
whose brand name
is half-erased
by the ancient sweat
of one thumb,
four fingers

11

Jack was in the water
& I was nearby

Kerouac was swimming among weeds & reeds
& I was dry. On a log

& there were others. & there was my daughter
eighteen months old, squatting on a log
& I saw her fall, my worst dream

I hurried in, no fear of the water
to find her
finally, under there & then
wake up

Wake up
Jack. It's you's
dead

12

The flying horse
                    catches fire
the red horse my
Thea rides. Who
                    placed her there

up on that beauty
                    on that fearsome
might. It drops
phosphorous bombs, it drops
who ever holds it loosely

its stable master
                    a tired cynical
old man named your honour

13

Her first black eye
just when Nixon is getting his

Who hit her they ask on the street

The world came by & did it

& who runs this world
indeed indeed indeed indeed, a vortex
that may come around
& slug you with a 38th parallel
any day of the week

What's this. Sunday

The swelling has just about
returned to normal

LETTER TO RICHARD NIXON

Open your hands
& let the States out

Open your hands, palms outward
& let the weapons & secrets
fall into the Capitol paper-shredder

Open your hand
& let Lorraine of France tickle your palm

she wants your attention for the night

she has no designs on the auto-parts plant in Michigan

The saying of its name makes the lips bitter
& leads to a humbling of the language

Open your hands & speak words
understood in the steam baths of Seattle

Open your hands & drop the arrows
drop the olive branch, drop the thunderbolt
drop the rigid lines around your mouth
loosen your tie, loosen your ties, Ecuador
will not break into the candy shop
when you turn your back, or if he does
let him gorge himself. Close your eyes & let Lorraine
rub your temples, release your scientists
from their lead aprons, let them make
rubbings on holiday temples in the Greek islands

Open your hands
& let the States out

Let them stay out after midnight, California
smooching in a car overlooking Pacific Standard Time Ocean

Massachusetts giving her virginity again
to a lover in a dinghy gently rockt by
Homer's latest waves

Quit looking at the clock, Dick

go to bed & listen to the radio
tune Virginia on the radio, she's
shucking corn & singing late at night, her lover
is at work also, the paper-shredder is eating
quietly thru the night. Drop your gray tie
into the paper-shredder, strip & jump into the pool
with Arkansas, a midnight swim, sunbathe
with the Black Panthers, sit side by side in rockers
with Marlon Brando, open your hands
& clap them enthusiastically as Chile balances the budget

Open your hands
& feel the strain leave your forearms

That is America coming home
a little drunk, happily singing
"We're engaged, she says she'll marry me

I'm going to make you a happy
grandfather at last"

14

Those unsustained—Saviours—
Present Divinity

staring from the magazine picture
in black pajamas

his eyes—had they met hers
would she recoil

into the closet perhaps
where her dresses hang now?

One hopes one
hopes not. They are

children's eyes, who have suffered
& come unto thee

Be ready to marry them, darling

15

Summer comes, I catch myself
peering down curbs, staring at silver grills
for strange licence plates
the gawdy colours of California ...

Oh poet! Numbers, numbers, your tawdry
body count, & those rich old women
with a cute name on their plate

What are you going to do
with your pocket full of stones

insult a lieutenant in mufti?

          Please, I say, leave me
logic, leave me my petty hate, poetry
doesnt hurt all that much, not
whom we would hurt it with

There are manuscripts of rice paper
in some crater floors, dirty
half-afloat, a char of Washington
on the corners, a usable dollar

It takes a hundred & fifty of those
to buy a windshield

16

For life and death, for the Body and for the eternal Soul,
Lo, I too am come, chanting the chant of battles,
I above all promote brave soldiers.

but offer no stripes, no dead-man's ears
no celebrations on the general's lawn

my soldiers wear bare arms like medals

musing in the grass of my skinny home town
lazing between forays, books by their sides
calling each other friend & fragging

any car that weighs more than 2,000 pounds

17

At war with the U.S.

I surrender

I embrace you

Now
get off my back

Stand
in the light
where I can see you

18

"Well I dont understand any of this
at all"

Oh dear

I dont, I
dont know what to do about that

I wish
you peace

19

I never knew what they meant
when they talkt about being deprest, now
I'm down in it, the dirty walls reach higher
& crumble when I scratch at them

Even the smallest things make me ponder suicide

The café I went to specifically for real french fries
today disht them out of the frozen bag

You nighted states I know you
are responsible for this, & I know
if I sprawl dead a minor martyrdom

the bowling alley coffee shop will be
mixing scum into the ground beef patties
in McCook Nebraska while they
take my corpse away &
puzzle my baby daughter's frowned-over eyes

20

Her innocence

I feed off that

I am so greedy for her
life. It's so hard

to come back, throw away
your life at the typewriter.

Rather toss with her
on the living room rug

go back, read the old poems
while she's asleep abed

while you are, separate historian

21

I am no maker

what is left is ashes

of whatever fire, what ever
was consumed

To go on
is the act, what is left

is always changing
too

Cinders of a poem

cinders of a body
killed for ferocious love

22

Stroking the melody

who has time
for this

when there are
bodies in the forest—

is that the music
heard only
when the jets
are turned off?

Fourth of July, 1973

23

When the war is over
there wont be any more newspapers

How long will it be
till we bomb our forests
into the year's final edition

Read old copies of Homer

read the Bible

study war no more

24

The lovely lines of war

the angry spaces of peace—

I am of two minds

Clinging to corpus callosum

the poet's lifeline

25

1944 I loved
the beautiful American army helmet

Naked, shining, drab, olive green
or painted with wide white stripes, maybe MP
or covered with netting, maybe leaves stuck all over
or a star on front for a *pistolero* general in fatigues
or dark blue in the battleship gun turret
or lying alone on the island beach sand in *Life* magazine

There's no more *Life* magazine
But the American helmet lying alone
on the jungle floor is beautiful

26

What you depart from
is not the process

but "I dislike unrest"
said Purdon Clarke, more American, sixty years ago
than he knew

A bomb crater remains
a water-filled hole
year after year, we plow
around it, making change

for the Washington dollar

A hole in the ground is no tradition
but difficult to distinguish
from the asshole
that dropt it

27

Yesterday
the young man with one leg
was on Broadway
in the latest summer styles

a young woman with him
looking to the few
churrs

He's paid up
he thinks, no mortgage
to hold him down

They had to destroy his body
to save it

28

In the unfamiliar
hospital room

she says
for the first time

Hi, Grampy

29

The Khmr
field hospital's
red cross is an American
target

where bombs will leave
holes no longer
filled with the most
resentful

Save my child

ready to receive
her North
American education

30

Two Greek kids across the street
shoot a ping pong ball
back & forth
with cheap plastic toys

Neither has caught it yet
but they persist
they persist

it is a game
& the gadgets are designed
for that one thing

31

The tears she brings from me
when we are alone

with her little
language. A dissolving

a salt where an alkali had been

There are still those
who tell me be tough

remember killing & who needs
killing. Nobody needs killing, nobody

I who gave her death
at the end, know, & know
my own, that I not see it never

32

It is a little plastic toy
the President has given them

Hey Joe

you got gum?

33

Now the Greek kid across the street
is carrying a stick, a rifle, over his right shoulder
American-style

& marching, his voice
like my drill corporal, 1954

Now it is a mortar
he sets in the forest
of his front yard

Where did that come from
his expertise

We were in NATO, no
nationalism, Greece is in NATO

no place for children

34

August 15, 1973, a day, they say
for the future. The B-52s are ordered
to stop dumping on Cambodia

My last day in the Greek neighbourhood

They're threatening to throw my daughter
out of school, 22 months of age
& she wont sleep in their room
full of beds

Way to go, trouble-makers!

Let me fail you no more
than I can support

than the blue hemispheres
hope for & deserve

Allophanes

Burnaby and Vancouver
1974–1975

(Coach House, 1976)

I

The snowball appears in Hell
every morning at seven.

Dr Babel contends
about the word's form, striking
its prepared strings
endlessly, a pleasure
moving rings outward thru
the universe. All
sentences are to be served.

You've tried it & tried it
& it cant be done, you
cannot close your ear—

i.e. literature
must be thought, now.

Your knee
oh
class
equal
poet
will like use a simile because he hates
ambiguity.

The snowball says it:
all sentences are imperative.

II

The culture
    tastes just like roast pig.

Here in what are not,
       never were, the “Outer Continents”

    where the buried ikons
are scattered throughout the soil we walk over,
paths hardly worn.

          Myths communicate
          with each other, & men
          seldom find out.

          The writing finger moves on
          & the sentence continues.

Archaeology is random, snow castles
are alright for lyric poems.

Being ventures us. A stolen base
wasnt there before you reacht it.

      Now it is real as a newspaper
         headline in Hell.

III

Fold the page before the ink dries
    & read before you pass on.

    Literature must be thought now.

There is no perspective
    when the eye is transparent.
When the author dies
    I disappear.

Companionship is true growing up,
    I reach for the companionship of art.

•

Ego dominus tuus? Oh, yeah, who are you?

"I am thy god of love."

Teh! I do not love litrachure,
books are my companions,
we grow old together,
we will never meet in Hell.

And you think *this* life is lonely!

Among earth, sky, mortals, divinities,
the obscure lies necessary to the luminous,
to make seeking take place of the random,
random, passive, the mental, lose it, Bubby,
spirits rejoice!
    the snowball is not the cold.
The free-standing flame is seen in the pool
you enter with your last wet page.

The work is henceforth

the author dead

the book, beside you

a face of the world

to which it was always leading

IV

Literary deciphering is not clarified butter.

By the help of an image
I call to my own opposite, summon all
that I have handled least, least lookt upon.

Have a seat on my language,
& here we go,

lecherously, thru the flowing world
of Hera's clitoris.

With a neoclassical
Neal Cassady, what a driver!

How do we get from the north pole
to the south pole?

& what would a snowball
know about polar knowledge?

Drive right past that lady, that's
St. As Is.   No, lady, sorry, my mother
says I gotta come home write a god damn poem.

Look, the big fellow just served her
some *cœur flambé.*

If you speak in tongues this trip, companion,
may I listen in ears?

v

"Talk to me of originality
    and I will turn on you with rage."

Open me not to find a beating heart
    but the irregular book of my people.

Hell is filled with those who have
    lost the good of the intellect.

Lost their *parole vide,*
    unable to serve their sentences in the dark.

Whatever I learned has run wild.

I awake in a hospital
under a patchwork quilt.

I underwent the operation of language
& wake in the recovery room.

As the colours stitch together
before my eyes.

As St. Arte is my bedside nurse

in a snow white skirt.

VI

I havent got a Dante's chance in Hell.

That snowball's got red stitches
        & it's imitating God.
Tells me from third to home
        is The Way Down And Out.

(Aw poet, just tell us how you
        felt about something.)

                What?
You dont want the untying
that frees the mind?

Dionysus is the power in the tree.
—like a Louisville Slugger.

There is safety in derision,
read either way.

        Sacredness of the act of thought
is transferred to the record, books made from trees,
& there it is, unmelting literature.

(Oedipus at Kelowna)

I woke to find the others gone,
six men working round the camp,
& I alone inside the tent,
I alone to meet the boss.

I'm too far north to run into the wood
where wisdom floods out work & fear.

VII (labour, life, literature) (the gods)

Keeping your eye on Satan's dewlap
you seek my complicity (

And when, amid no earthly moans
Down, down that town shall settle hence,
Hell, rising from a thousand thrones,
Shall do it reverence.

) in this watching in
this (?) madness

/ Hermes & Aphrodite
face to face
coupling again
on the far side
of the moon

I have loved you better than my soul
for all my words, else why be we here?

You'll join in burying my poem
at some crossroads.

Aw narrative
is a telling blow.

Tell the story of men,
their progress on Earth,
a cancer on her body.

This is depressing salt I stand in, I sink.

The egg sits there,
it does not rot itself.

Watch the three-year-old
walk thru the gate
carrying her own lunch bucket.

A burden I cant stand to carry
as I must rattle my head & body
to break the pictures of my
cooperating, dying father.

An other, that close,
an other, &
that near, an other.

& where has Maud gone?

Here I am,
all over.

VIII

Does not the eye altering alter all?

It is a spilled ice cream ball,
kick it to hell & Gone,
& turning the cone over,
place it on your head.

Stay above ground that way.

You get a headache &
germs scatter to the ends of the earth,

Oh sages standing in God's holy shit.

She crouches
over the fire,
her back curved
to her care,

child watching
from his wrappings
in the dark.

IX

How embarrassing, said Mr Auden
finding himself still awake at midnight.

The traffic control operator in Byzantium
always takes time for lunch
to munch the cooled flesh
of some gray sheep.
The one o'clock gong
just tells him what time it is.

The dead are breathless
& so am I
alive

going at times
where they are.

Strange names,
a phonebook of the damned.

Vein frenzy awoke & he died.

The winds scatter fragments of the exploded gods.
Fall leaves blowing about one's feet.
Cross yourself.
Burn the books.

Desire is not hunger,
desire makes it impossible to eat anything.

I will always want to open a veil before beauty one day

& next day melt it down with coarse salt.

(pluck the melting sno-cone of the lightbulb)

X

Et verbum cano factum est .

A large invisible hand is spinning those wheels Ezekiel sees.

But the flesh became chops.

History, history, its range adds to our being,
not our knowledge, history
is a shadow of myself cast upon the stream of time.
The world's meaning is the shadow of the gods,
passing one another, in commerce, in furious battle.

Those cast out are without shadow, without words.

See the word made white & melting
before the turn of the fiery wheel.

I see the dog licking it up,
he turns & goes home, *cano mirabilis.*

—I do believe that Eblis hath
a snare in every human path—

The world's meaning is exactly
fol de rol de rolly O .

(Put the contraries
back into mortal life,

fail at suicide,
barely.

—burn the books
burn the books

Stamp the snow off your boots
onto the face of the rug.

XI (the egg-ziled gods)

(*Run for the roundhouse, Nellie, he cant corner you there.*)

Sea spray crashes on the temple
& sets it aflame.

Wear your best suit
when you jump into a volcano.

You would sweep me away
into an indefinite world
that fills me with terror!

Shuffle: courage & power
knowledge & pleasure

fire

air  water

earth

Al "Chemical" Rose
Has quick hands
& a strong throwing arm

I had gathered about me all gods
because I believed in none.

Every time the peacock raises the mirror breaks
in "numberless" pieces & the world
must be re-distilled.

If you don't understand the story you'd better tell it.

Damn a people who cant handle or be handled
by more than a single god. Those slaves, those wisps.

XII

There is no system, Al Rose falls into an easy chair
brought for relaxation into the laboratory.
His thought threatens him, it is
the perilous deterioration of dynamite.
It is the pattern of snowballs
thrown against a maroon wall.

Dionysus crucified on a wheel,
stupefied in a Kelowna vineyard.

His gods speak no man's language,
what arrogance, the churchmen would hear their "voices."
One sees their messages in the reeds.

Read his thoughts as experts sift thru an airplane's
wreckage.

Oh God, let's have war, fuck art, that
phony lastingness, shoot him in the belly,
blood is vintage, there'll be another
crop, the vines will plunge into
the earth, fanatics will raise another.

Why should men die & books live?

•

On TV we sat breathless as death,
watching them blast the top off the mountain,

to begin, to make a perfect earth, a perfect smooth black orb.

XIII

Do you believe all this stuff?

Man & the unthought are contemporary.
The unthought is not born of him or in him
but beside him.

Forget Hell,
                Heaven must be another, a camisole,
                must be what we don't want.
                What I want is baseball, jazz, & Viennese food.

                Credo quia absurdus sum

                Take off your shirt & let the sun burn.

My soul grows larger as it rolls downhill,
beauty grown sad with its eternity.

Thus.   Logos is true narrative,
Wild logos, mad skier. Al Rose intent on suicide,
His meaning left in lines on the melting snow.

The iconoclast preaches in his best clothes,
The pedagogue levels a burp-gun at his jacket buttons.

XIV

Al Rose: I have little reason.
Bachiller: To what?
A: What?
B: Little reason to what?
A: To wit.

A: History is the spirit made concrete.
B: With the odd window.
A: The odd balcony.

A: Is the self always gathering the undone to itself?
B: Yes.
A: No, it is always moving into the other,
removing its clothing as it goes.
B: You're only interested in the narrative of philosophy.

A: Yes.
B: Odd.

9

A: It takes time to centre in on a moving target.
B: I've never been moved much by a target.
A: To aim straight & tell the truth, that is our first virtue.

B: Nowadays we talk often of a gift, but with no idea of
a giver.
A: & teachers?
B: There is only learning.
A: Thoth was the great giver.
B: What we have is not a gift but a possession.
A: Yes, I suppose so. An image Monday.

XV

Hieros (marry, liquify)

Nothingness is a point
of departure. Choose becoming
over being, how do elsewise
& love thyself?

Hear a
dead face
laughing
centuries ago,
your kinsman.

The Doom of the Powers: all the planets
drop into the Sun.

Geronimo makes a great catch against the wall
& it melts in his hand.

& you think you can talk to the gods
in English?

Man is nature, devouring,
man is culture, fuelling language.

filling the hopper

The culture tastes like well-cookt pig.
The black pig in the valley.

[*prose gloss*: The numbing explosion of human population in the past decade has drawn God away from each man's need. How would the devils find the time to struggle over every soul?]

XVI

The Holy Gobbler

Morphemes fall in flames from the tree.

א

There was black fire writ on white fire,
the poem blazed before my very eyes.
I wanted to dive into the flames,
save my furniture,
rescue my "beloved books."

Al Rose speaks seventy languages fluently,
sings in seventy languages,
his words fall into the sun, athanor
too.

He looks away from the blaze
& a black fire meets his gaze.
A burning tree,
that speaks thru thee.

Bachiller says oh he is busy bullshitting about Heaven
& his pants are on fire. You watch,
you'll see him sitting in the snow.

God's holy name is at anyone's fingers,
any scrambler,
thank you, Mr Underwood.

XVII

Only dry or drying sticks can be tied into a bundle.

He's ninety years old & he sits reading in the pitch black night.

B: Pass him by, he's trying to do a number on us.
A: He'll freeze to death, he obviously needs help.
B: He gets heat the same place he gets light to read by.

A: I lookt down his throat & there was the whole universe!
B: His head was then above it.
A: Or cast out of it.

"What matter that you understand no word!
Doubtless I spoke or sang what I had heard
In broken sentences." The snowball appears
in Hell every morning at seven, fears
no fire more than time, the planets too
will fall into the sun & so will you
& so will you.

No place on Earth
is the centre of the world,

it is the centre of the world.

XVIII The fruitful void. Athanor.

One said he's been "trying to learn to use words
& every attempt is a wholly new start."

Where else may we find our beginnings
but in the language? The shepherd's song
on a hillside in the invaded sub-continent.
That native blows a pipe in our nature.
One is not born alone, one borrows the earth,
a clay, formed anew. A language filled again
in an oast heated from an ancient flame.

Build, though,
with snow,
blow language
nummular
at the flame.

When you've finisht with them words
throw the skins on the compost, will ya?

That is composition,
autobiologist.

The last kiss
is given to the void.

Bye bye, sweetheart.

Rome
was once the biggest city in the world.

Goodbye, Rome.

XIX *factum*

A little devotion

The spool turns faster the moment you begin to take your
eyes off it.

You slow it by watching.

—Thought is the action of the moment brought—
But it will take its time,
it will take no more time than it would.

(That is the fine étude of man.)

Pure poetry has no presence
but only its own being

250 years ago tomorrow
man stept out of nature
into history

Ideas fall,
peanut shells
blown by passing vehicles
along the gutter.

Dog turds
Discolouring the snow
About them.

A radiance.

Aw busker,
what dance is this
you tap before us?

Only, again "only"
the true beginning of
language is poetry.

Actualité.

XX

Where is the theology in all this?

There will be no recurrence of the pre-
reflective time of man.
            No recourse there,   (That him
                the fine étude   with the
of man walkt with him   big dick?)
            the moment he could stand.

"Neither baseball
nor poetry
is for fun."

Die, aspiration
Let the man bend over,
Make a snowball,

Joyful weapon made of water.
A kid's jape.
For the love of God.

Life & art are consubstantial.
    H.C.E.
    lives & lives & lives
    reflected in the mirrors
    along the wall.

Text, Criticism, & Notes.   Edited by George H. Bachellor.

XXI *Simon Magus*

Looking for an oblate snowball
on Eggs Isle.   Inside the real
composing.
                    A permanent place down in the universe
over which history
has no dominion.

                              This is not going,
anywhere, not going,
anywhere, not,
going, I dont seem to be,
going. Anywhere.

Exile & cunning. I flew
in my dream, night by night, standing
upright.

                                        I had no religious instructors,
                                        poor child, only a grandpa
                                        who'd once abandoned
                                                        the ministry.

            (They've already printed
                    the date of your death.

You wont be ready,
you'll say you have things to do,
you'll say it cant be done today.
He'll say that's what they all
say.)

I abandoned
the mystery.

I keep trying to bite my pencil with a tooth gone five years ago.

XXII

"He does what is done in many places;
what he does other
                he does after the mode
of what has always been done."

Not seeking to under
stand this world

(I am making)

but to put his hands
        into it, to continue
                shaping what he is.

•

"Chemical" Rose:

        His athanor was raised to lips
& lips at that First Supper.

        His familiar pranced beneath the board
ready to retrieve angelic orts.

        His dream lay on a carvèd plank
dropping petals into a cup.

        His tongue drips berry juice
onto his clean shirt front.

        His name is, discovered to be
Huckleberry Finnegan.

XXIII

I felt something strike me.
I fell on something.
With a shape something like my own.

The language
is not spoken,
it speaks.

Somewhere in the world you could have a green rose.

Language scales the real, & continues, on.

Oistrakh
touches
the fifth
string.

Move out of these too tight clothes
    when you feel the trance ending

    & I will tell you

history is a thing. A dead language
    in which all words
        describe, & refer,

you may understand history because you made it.

You will never understand nature
    because you are nature,

(Jan Garbarek,
blow.)
when you are able to shape the natural
history will vanish from your mind.

Drama
may not be superimposed.
It opens
before your chary feet.

Watch, that priest
looks up at us,
a snowball wouldnt melt in his mouth!

XXIV Diaspora

"All imaginable relations may arise between a man and his
God."

What off
was Thoth
but ne'erdowell
exprest.

Skill forgotten with age.
Oh dread! what enters
to fill that space?

(Shit, shore up the fragments
for yourself, dont expect
a fullness here, I'm only
one pair of ears.)

The effacement of words.
History is full of holes
thru which we may hope
to escape (?)

The artist has disappeared,
he is standing silent before God.
Wha'd you say? asks the latter.

I know, I know.
it's all beautiful.
Tell me what we said on it.

The bapdismal font
is full of words.

What fire forms
friday
theism?

Nature
to adventure
prest.

XXV

Here hope is always thwarted.
The future when we get there
is always other than we'd thought
& it is not the future.

Say to it:
"I trust the sufferings endured in battle
more than I trust you."

Today we go always to children's games & songs
to prove the real.
To try to drown poor pussy cat.

•

The blue fell,
the green rose

& I was prest between.

I lifted & threw something.
It struck something.
& fell in pieces on something like itself.

prose summary: The words proveth the Almighty the
greater thing to come along as yet.

XXVI Dispersoid

Pri, mord, Eos, reality
not the light brim again
rather sink
into the ooze

but she pulls
she weeps
we are really (surprise) gone from her
but she weeps

We see her
weeping
we are there
too

Bye, Mama
we are engaged.

Language rings us.

There was first the beauty of fucking.
Then the morality of fucking.
Now the fucking drama.
Here is the theology in all this.

It has melted in my hand.

Call me Mister Warm.

Smoking Mirror

Vancouver and Fredericton
1979

(Longspoon, 1982)

1 SMOKING MIRROR

The more I stare
into the smoking mirror
the more I no longer see what's
there behind me.

Who is holding
the smoking mirror, who
leapt out of the water
to be baptised?

Who is teaching me
to climb down to heaven
to fall upward to
my reflection?

Who instructed me
that dissolving skin
reveals my proper covering
in the hour of my baptism?

This moment was brought to me
on the burning water
it was shown to me
in the smoking mirror.

2 THE FOOTPRINT

The one holding
the smoking mirror
left his footprint
on my face.

I am directed to point out
the morning lake
with vapour
rising from it.

Look into its surface
for reflection, see
the fate of your life
there, steamed away.

The print fades
from my cheek, I
must flay myself
to keep it.

So that lake, the sun
climbs higher in
the sky, the steam
goes with your glance.

I can direct you
no further, you reflect
only in the morning,
by noon you are
far from the shore.

3 THE FOUR CORNERS

It is in the brain's shared work
we discover the music

singing at the heart
of every thing

its movement pictured
this way:

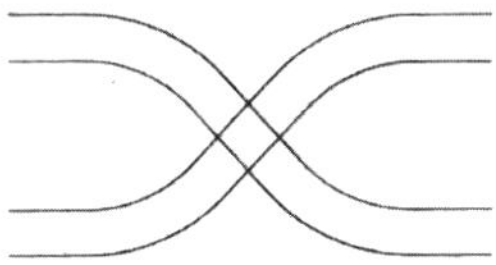

(THAT IS SHARED)

The four corners
in confluence, the brain

distributing, likewise
its intelligence, only to be
realized at the centre.

•

So the city, under
influence of its four suns

must be visited in all
its daily seasons

to find the centre.
A camera set on the mountain

& left to run, will see four
not the fifth sun.

4 BEFORE THE REVOLUTION

Before the revolution
we lie in one another's earth
dreaming of the past, bananas
floating north, hate
floating south, our arms
the heat of home.

The black face hate learned
from brown & white, Cortés
as rich as United Fruit
& Spanish to boot. Our own

priests singing at the
Iroquois stake. It is so lovely
to think we grew without
armed overthrow. Oh yes.

I have waited 300 years for Asia
to come across the archipelago
& they have not come,
bombs for you, Asia, a new
tax plan for us, we all have to suffer
in our various ways.

Am I not clear? It is clear
as the historical data
for boundaries, the boardwalk
in Québec City, for instance,
hardly ever felt the touch
of deerhide shoes.

Before the revolution
there is order, the red face
in the capitol is apoplexy,
the red face under the cliff
is history.

5 THE WATER FLAME

The smoking mirror
flows around
a protuberance of clarity—

It is
fire risen from the water,
it is the heart of the earth
hoping to be free
from its death.

It is my heart
defying the haze at the surface
to break free
summoning its own flow.

Fire from smoke,
the mirror no longer desired.
It is not to seek reflection
but to burn
we must strive.

Smoke gone, there is
clarity, my blood
burst thru the skin!

6 OPEN MIND

Oh yes, yellow door
opens at last into my own skull
where the rooms are joined
by glass bead curtains.

Walking around in here
I stumble on my old friends
lying in the shadows
on the floor.

They tell me there are things
in here I'll never know,
secrets they've learned
in the thick smoke of their dreaming.

Not to envy them, not to
envy them—there are ways
to friendship that dont need
your total understanding.

I run my hand among the beads
thinking of barter, myself
a hesitant Cortés, eyeing
those Indians on the floor.

But the yellow door admits
no religion, it takes an
open mind to enter
a filled up head.

7 DIỆM'S MACHINE

Diệm's portable guillotine
moved from village to village
distributing summary justice.

Now the heads of the hamlets
fall to other
non-Frenchmen. Ah, clever

place for war, for national
liberation, for agrarian reform
of the mind. I have never been

to Asia, I should say
nothing about it. I have been
to the U.S. consulate, I

have seen the heavy faces looking out,
the paper cups of coffee,
& my feet were cold except

for the marching, that done south-
ward far from this shore,
I hear the fall of those feet,
those heads.

8 FREDERICTON HOUSES

Fredericton houses
are wooden, frames

of bright paint
                    in hard snow
beside the fro-
zen river.

Bright? In the hard
sun: green, pink, & yellow.

It is my first time
in Fredericton, I dont
watch the houses long enough

to see the dark people,
I dont watch the river

long enough to see the dark
water
        confidently moving
from under the ice.

9 SMOKING MIRROR IN FREDERICTON

I move these Maritime children
with my stories of
the smoking mirror.

I see a foggy reflection
in their eyes, panels
of forgotten Kanada.

The Saint John morning paper
has sixteen pages, two of them
for local obituaries.

(Am I bringing their hidden fate
from public legend?
The eyes have it.)

The eyes have it,
& they wont let go.

10 SMOKING MIRROR IN ALBERTA

It is the smoking mirror
I carried from México
in my pocket to Calgary.

I know enough not to tell
the Blood Indian at his public table
your cousin built the largest city
in four continents.

We tied him to a wheel, we
Europeans, crossing an ocean
we saw the bright reflections
of our flagships in the water.

Kerrisdale Elegies

Vancouver
1981–1982

(Coach House, 1984)

Here a star, and there a star,

Some Lose their way.

Here a mist, and there a mist:

Afterwards—day!

—Emily Dickinson

In the night the wind slides in from the sea
and eats at our faces;
                                        that sweetheart,
she would do anything you ask her,
ask her,
                she'll lie down for a lonely heart.
Nighttime's for lovers, maybe, closing their eyes
and pretending tomorrow will be splendid.

You should know that, you adult;
why dont you fling your arms wide
into the juicy air, chuck your ardent loneliness,
bump birds out of their dark paths
homeward to their grieving chicks.

Be grateful—
sadness makes music, cruel
April tuned a string for you.
Moons
whirled around planets waiting for you to spot them.
The middle of the Pacific prepared a wave
to plash ashore at your visit.
A radio
switched to melody as you walked by
a neighbour's window.

You should know by now,
the world waited
to come alive at your step—
could you handle that?
Or did you think this was love,
movie music
introducing a maiden you could rescue?
Where were you going to keep her,
and keep her
from seeing those dreams you were already
playing house with?

When your heart hungers,
sing a song of six-
teen, remember your own maidenly love
and the girls that aroused it,
make them famous.
Remember their plain friends who danced so well
because they never got into a back seat.
Bring them all back, become a lyric poet again.
Identify with heroes who die for love
and a terrific image,
you'll live forever
in your anguished exalted metaphors.
Oh yeah.

But remember nature?
                                        She takes back all
worn-out lovers,
                              two lie in the earth, one moulders
above ground;
                           nature is an exhausted mom,
she cant go on forever,
                                        this is late
in the machine age.
                                   Can you think of one woman
who gave up on the stag line and turned
to God and a peaceful lawn?

Isnt it about time we said to hell with agony?
Shouldnt we be rich with hit-parade love by now?
Arent we really free to choose joy over drama,
and havent we come through looking pretty good,
like a line-drive off a perfect swing
in the ninth inning?
                                        It leaves the bat faster
than it came to the plate.
                                                  Taking that pitch
and standing still in the batter's box is nowhere.

Somebody's talking.
                                        Listen, stupid Kerrisdale heart,
the way your dead heroes listened, till
they were lifted out of their shoes,
but they couldnt hear it all, they thought
they were standing on earth.
                                                        No,
you're not going to hear the final clap of truth;
that would kill you in two heartbeats.

But listen to the wind in the chestnut trees,
the breath of autumn's bleeding,
                                        the death
of your young heroes.
                                You recall the breeze
across from the station in Florence
where you saw an amazing name by the door?
Remember the clouds pulled off the face
of Mont Blanc you saw from the morning window?
Why would the wind reach down to me?

Am I supposed to translate that swishy voice
into some kind of modern law?
Make me their liar even as the chestnuts are?

Déesse dans l'air répandue,
Flamme dans notre souterrain!

Yes, I know, it is odd to be away from the world,
dropping all the habits you learned so well;
never bending to look at a rose face to face,
throwing your name away,
free of hands that held you fiercely,
laughing at what you once ached for,
watching all the old connections unravel in space.

Being dead is no bed of roses,
you have so much work piled up in front of you
before the long weekend.
But the folks who are still alive are too quick
to make their little decisions.
The spooks, they tell me, cant tell whether they're moving
among corpses or the fretful living.
The everlasting universe of things rolls
through all minds of all ages in every back yard,
and none of them can hear themselves think.

The ones who left early don't need our voices;
they're weaned from this ground as neatly
as we're diverted from Mom's tit. But
what about us?
                                        We need the mystery, we need
the grief that makes us long for our dead friends,
we need that void for our poems.
We'd be dead without them.

Queen Marilyn made silly movies, but she's
the stuff our words are made from.
                                        Her meaning
struts along the lines of a hundred lovely books.
Her music may be heard in the gaps in the traffic
of 41st Avenue.
                    Her shiny breasts
fill the hands of our weeping poets.

ELEGY TWO

Dead poets' voices I have heard in my head
are not terrifying.
They tell me like lovers
we are worth speaking to,
I am a branch
A singing bird will stand on for a moment.

Like a singing branch I call out in return. How
do otherwise?
Rather that than couple
with a swan on 41st Avenue.
When Hilda
appeared in my dream, she did not visit, she
walked by, into the other room,
and I didnt fall
in fear, but in love.

Inside.

Out there was the fortunate fall, mountains
glistening with creation,
                                        a glacier between them,
flowing bright out of the working god's fingers,
first orchards rising from the melt, light
shaped on crest and cut,
                                        the roll of storms
shaking new trees, flattening the grass,
                                                            quick lakes
a scatter of mirrors, clouds in them, all
favour, all breathing side to side, all
being outside,
                        all blossom.

As for us, we dissolve into hungers,
                                                            our breath
disappears every minute,
                                              our skin flakes off
and lies unseen on the pavement.
                                                         She says
I've got you under my skin, yes, she says
you walk with me wherever I go,
                                                         you are
the weather.

                    I reply with a call for help,
I'm disappearing,
                              there's a change in the weather.

Half the beautiful ones I have known are gone,
what's the hurry?
On this street the school girls
grow up and disappear into kitchens,
a breeze
shakes the blossoms from my cherry tree,
there's cat hair all over the rug.
What happened
to that smile that was on your face
a minute ago?
God, there goes another breath,
and I go with it,
I was further from my grave
two stanzas back, I'm human.
Will the universe
notice my unattached molecules drifting thru?

Will the dead poets notice our lines appearing among them,
or are their ears filled with their own music?

Will their faces look as blank as these I pass
on 41st Avenue?
I'm not talking about
making that great anthology,
I am recalling that god
who said excuse me, I wasnt listening, sorry.

In love we have a secret language we dont remember.
We catch a word or two,
                                        as the wind passes,
we turn an ear to the cool,
                                           it's gone. The trees
shake their leaves to say look,
                                                we're alive.
The house you've sat in for years remains
against all odds,
                          a part of the earth.

We are the wisps,
                             we flit invisible
around all that wood.
                                   They dont even hear us,
they may be waiting for us to say something important.

Late night on 37th Avenue I see lovers
on each other in a lamplit Chevrolet.

Do their hands know for certain that's skin
they glide over?
                    I have rubbed my neck in exhaustion,
and almost believe I've touched something.

Is that a reason to look forward to next year?
Still, being dead
is no bed of roses.

But the moony flesh in the sedan
turns like the firmament,
                                        he is entangled
in legs and gearshift,
                                    she likely says yes
and grows to meet his growth,
                                            dumb imitation
of the burgeoning garden in the nearby yard.

I grow more frail as they fill the car,
already disappearing,
                                    should I ask them
whether I exist?

Si me soubmectz, leur serviteur
En tout ce que puis faire et dire,
A les honnorer de bon cuer

I know they put their hands there and there
because their early fancy now arrives,
                                                            an island
risen from a placid sea.
                                          An actual breast, a leg
that does not disappear below conflicting pictures.

But the ones who have touched me have
disintegrated into seraphs and books.

These half-undressed in the front seat
have nearly slipped from time,
                                                  elastic hours
making Pleiades of the street.

Yet if they see the morning,
                                                            safe from their first
rough sea,
                        if they smooth each other's hair,
talk about their weekend shopping—are they
what they were?
                                  Are they as far from time?

Do they kiss, and try to kiss again, and say
inside, yes I remember this?
                                                              Does a mask
feel the touch of a mask;
                                                      does the face
beneath the mask feel the mask?

Did you see ancient Fred and whitened Ginger
in the morning paper,
                                        June 25, 1982? Now
each time we see them glide by each other's
garments in black & white youth, we stand
amazed.
              How light that touch, how quick,
how foreign to dull surge of our own passion,
we thought.
                    They generated enormous energy, yet
met like eyelashes.
                              They were exactly like us.

God, should he choose,
                                        can press us into
sausage patties,
                         he can flatten a car,
furl up a street,
                         tuck us into our own shoes.

We step out of cars, finally,
movies come to an end,
we need a place at last that will fit us,
we need a cabin, a creek, a few trees,
maybe a typewriter and a sink.
We are evaporating
as our heroes did.
We cannot pursue our fragments
as they separate into earth and stars.

ELEGY THREE

Love is yearning for the stars,
                                        love is yearning
by the night stars for a body full of blood.

Send a dozen love poems into the late air
and where are you?
                              The deep shame in the body,
The ancient, rude-formed cave god in the blood
She may suspect but never see;
                                          he blushes with hunger
she knows nothing about.

What a vulnerable thing she is
in her crisp white summer dress.

He swims noisily in his black red ocean,
grunting and blowing,
a comic book horror of a sea lion.

His snorting echoes off the rocks
ashore.
The night sky appears and recoils,
the stars
move back an inch.
They smile in their own
surrounding dark,
they know themselves.
In a moment
He is a gentle swain looking like a sky
Into her accepting eyes.

Thou art lightning and love, she says,
but the hunger in his face is not for her, nor
was it given at his birth.
                                        His thick lips
around your nipple, girl, are not sucking you alone.

You are a wisp,
                          your sudden coming moves him
only to the beginning of his passion,
                                                  he is in you,
yes, and now he is thru you.

True, you caught his breath with your fingers,
but that groan you heard,
                                        that frightened lunge
ran across the ether and up his spine,
                                                        he's gone.

Say his name and only his corpse will reply.
Only his body and the nearest part of his soul
will make a home in your warmth.

He is your child,
                            except for the dark area behind his eyes,
he will grow in your garden,
he will be new for you.

He was new for his Kerrisdale mom,
he grew
like a poppy in her garden.
She kept him in after dark,
safe from midnight vapours.
He was her
riddle of bones.
She was his tidy doorway,
keeping him safe,
showing him his new world
a little at a time.
She gave him a wooden gun
when he was eight.
She read him stories
in which children win
but grew up anyway.

She held him in the middle of her own slight spasm,
a magnesium flash that swallowed the shadow
behind the door,
                                        the shadow that looked around then
just like his adult body today.
                                                                        Stars
cast faint but ineradicable shadows.

Curtains can be drawn by Mom
before she goes to her own bed.

Lying in the dark becoming lighter he scents the perfume
he knows also from your purse,
he feels
the approach of his other mother sleep,
this family
is sweeter than anything he will know,
he is safe, you think;
but where he is going
someone is typing up the code for the first
season of the world.
You see he sleeps, a
passive vacancy present here,
he sleeps,
but he dreams too;
and where he now soars
there are no mothers,
there are only
stellar monsters to be loved,
there are galaxies
of fire just missing the cockpit.
He is inside,
where you have been but can never enter.

He loves the terror prior to earth life.
                                                                        You
would hate it if you knew.
                                                        He loves
the collapsing bridge he is running upon.

In his dreams inside his dreams he knows he will
make it,
                    step to the edge of green ground
the moment the crash will sound.
                                                                You smile
at his rolling eyelids as you back out of his room.

He's back again among the gruesome beings
who welcome him,
                    who smile with bleeding lips,
whose eyes search him out,
                              whose ancient brittle eyes
he smiles into.
               Before you turn
you see a smile fleet on his face.
                              Your heart
warms as you walk downstairs to your vegetables.

You love his dream you do not know.
                                   He
is among the dreadful ancestors he knew
before you felt him kick inside your womb.

The young woman steps from the car,
                                        her feet
among flowers.
                    She thinks she is a new love.

But we do not love anything new.
                                        You lift
in me a cool green earth,
                              home of all my dead loves,
a blonde Pictish girl of unexplainable beauty,
glimpsed on her daily walk in my farthest sleep,
a sea of dead sailors,
                         the valley of their mothers,
my heart filled with living voices
heard by the ears of Cygnus.
                                   Last winter
on the train thru Carrara I heard them
for a second,
                  and the train is running today.

As I watch you walk,
                         your white dress
falling around your thighs in the starlight,
I love you for everybody you have been.

I don't care whether your mother is waiting up for you.

Mother, you have lovers too,
                                        they stir in their armour.

The flush you feel comes from ancient eyes on your back.

Men are beating each other below Mount Cyllene
for the right to bring you an asphodel.

Widows detest you,
                                their grown children lust for you.

A gentle painter caught you
in that quattrocento oil you saw in Florence last December.

When he comes downstairs in the morning,
his eyes
asquint against the window light,
bring his berries
from the yard,
hug him for the warmth from his bed,
promise him an afternoon at the beach.

The stars will be out of the sky
till long past supper time.

ELEGY FOUR

These high chestnut branches along Larch Street
fade above the streetlights,
                                        live without me.

A truck passes in the morning,
                                              it is full summer,
and a flock of noisy starlings leaps into the sky.

I jump from my top step,
                                      and sprawl on the lawn,
eyeglasses bouncing twice along the walk.

I dont know what time of year it is,
                                                     I flower
and die each afternoon.
                                    A muscular dog trots by,
certain where he's going.

I follow one scent,
sure of my appetite,
but am distracted by a crossing spoor.
My nature
is torn,
I am a trespasser,
I promised to
steer clear,
stay in my own territory,
but love
makes intruders,
I am not here,
but the burglar
of your past.

“I” dont even see you till the light blinks
and a white backdrop appears behind you.

It hurts the eye that turns to rest on you.

Inside I am a blind mystery,
                                        only my skin
knows what is happening.

I've stood before the oven door my heart
is baking in, wondering,
how will it come out?

Will it burn before the buzzer goes,
will silly images fill my anxiety waiting here?

When I take it out will it make the guests
go ahh,
another Kerrisdale satisfaction?

The trees outside the kitchen window
know the shape of the wind in their roots,
and I'm standing here,
sniffing for smoke.

What am I doing in the kitchen?

I'd rather be upstairs with my toys.
                                        I know
how they work.
                    I don't mind their fake colours.

I'll spend hours with my toy trucks,
play in the dark,
                    listen to the hiss of the trees.

I dont care whether my spooky ancestors
sit on the floor with me,
                              gruesome beings.

They can remain the other side of the collapsing bridge
between those stars,
                         they can call me over,
I don't care.
               Here I stay.

                              I can listen to them
like a radio in the dark.

At my father's funeral I held my mother's hand
and my sister's fierce hand,
                                        and heard my father's voice.

It's all right, the words in my quiet head,
it's all right,
          and I half believed him,
                              half believed
them.

     I was born dead centre of the depression,
grew up watching him settle for less,
                              watching him
read less as time wore on and there was more real furniture.

I spent hours with him devoid of speech,
carrying wood, throwing a ball, flipping a card
hours growing an attachment that would not speak.

I speak to him now in all my poems,
                                                            my body
speaks to him every time I look at it.
                                                            He is silent,
aware of my ambition but as in my childhood
tolerant of my forms.
                                            Asking only that I know work,
that I come to his station;
                                                  so I remember his calling
each time I toil unbidden in the yard.

It's all right.

Upstairs with my toys—a pen, some lined paper,
my books open around me.

I am staring at this sound
coming out blue, so hard,
another voice
must mix with its own,
a dead poet or father.

So there are three of us,
who divide the world
by remaining apart,
come together on these
rare occasions,
funeral of the trees
(one voice said this,
the others assented in the saying).

The gruesome gone hear us in moments like this,
the wheel descending to their chambers.
They laugh
derisively,
they know how seldom we come together.

They know that we will walk apart
for most of the year.
We court them thus
and they say "nice try,"
though by then we are gone again,
back to the kitchen,
back to the grave,
back into a book more often mentioned than open.

My childhood's toy never grew cool from my gone touch.
They were presents,
                                        they had no history but mine.
They fell into shapes on the floor,
                                                                constellations
observed in Cathay and Tical.
                                                        Voices murmured around them.

They would disappear when I learned
to buy my own books.
I was in no hurry to grow,

                                                    or so I thought,
                                                                        but I moved
                                                                  to where the stars
were fewer,
                        I carried my books and magazines with me.

I was always the youngest and the best read.
I wanted not to please my elders but to annoy them,
by exceeding their speed,
                                                by leaping
  past their adulthood,
                                            child's skin on my face.

Most of all I loved my solitude,
hoping another
somewhere did the same,
and another somewhere
between toys and the world soon to be made.

I knew my solitude was pictured between stars,
knew a long-dead vizier read it on a screen
and approved,
as no parent could.

Déjà l'odeur bouge en des orages gonflés
Suinte sous le pas des portes
Aux chambres secrètes et rondes,
Là où sont dressés les lits clos.

Can I show you that sole child behind his own door?
Point to where he rides between two stars
considering his path?

                                        Is it I who has to
whiten his hair,
                              narrow his arteries, perhaps
put a bullet between his shoulders?
                                                            That could be
easy, lock me up,
                              forget what cell I'm in.

But each step he takes before he thinks of walking
is a step toward the grave,
                                                a step down
into the earth.

                         He carries his shroud with him
on the first day of school.

                                              Think of that
And ask for a book of musical thought!

ELEGY FIVE

For a few hours,
for a summer,
we think we know them,
these young men in three-coloured caps,
playing
the game of boyhood,
brief in our eyes.

So they play for us,
or are they performing
the ancient demands of their decorated bodies?

They wear their names on their backs,
but they wear costumes designed a century past,
of gentlemen meeting of a Sunday on the grass.

The white ball acts upon them as a stone in a pool.
They run, they bend, they leap, they fall
to the patchy green carpet,
walled away from the factory city.

The eye up high for a moment catches
a soft human Diamond,
                                        a star
twinkt in a moment by the hurl, the ex-
stacy of the thing among them.

                                                    The giant at first
leaps then tumbles,
                                his feet quick to return
to artificial earth.

                             What holds him there
is not anywhere.

The crowd opens,
rises like a row of poppies,
and subsides,
scattering peanut shells like petals.

They surround the never-dying game,
a stem that feeds their seeming boredom,
the late innings,
the mom at home
basting a roast.
Children stray thru the stands,
faces away from the centre.

A thin fine play in the eighth
draws a flutter of hands.

The wrinkled neck of the third base coach
mocks his uniform,
                                        or vice versa.
He wears no spikes,
                                        but shoes like slippers.
His stomach falls over his double-knit belt.

His statistics lie like the skeleton of another man
in yearbooks out of print.

He never stands in the coach's box, as if
afraid it might be a grave.

Beauty is the first prod of fear,
                                        the young
shortstop knows it but does not say it.
                                                  Tobacco
bulges his cheek,
                    his movement speaks
of his parentage,
                    a swan and a gangster.

He is simple for three hours.

He knows the ground between his feet.

You play thru your injuries,
                                        you play
hurt,
        you knew it was waiting for you,
you remember your first bad arm,
it said your pension would be full of pain.

You hit the ground every day,
knocked over in the middle of your grace,
a green apple hitting every branch
on the way to the sun-beaten orchard floor;

your team-mates' play called it into being,
                                                            your fall
seen a hundred times on the screen,
a way down, and out.
                                    You bounce up
without a smile,
                        but the crowd says "ahh,"
and you look quick at your manager,
                                                Dad,
were you watching me.

                                    He is looking in his book,
but your sore body grins
all the way back to the dugout,
unaware of your steps over the grave.

Already the stands are noisy
with the call for some hitting,
                    the home half
cuts the pain from your knees,
                    your heart
hides in the shade,
                hoping the pitcher
will serve unwritten fate,
                  your wooden friend
will find a fatness,
                you will run
to throw yourself to earth again,
                    let me in.

Baseball angel,
                    it's early summer,
                                        accept him,
lighten the air,
                    open the infield,
                                        give him
one white rainbow today,
                              set him on second,
the lovely red dirt all over his flannel.

Extra
basis.

And shine bright shadows on the tan skin
of that sweetheart with the odd designation:
ball girl.

I watch her blossom these years,
call her Debbie though I don't know her;

she sits in a simple folding chair next to the stands,
glove on her hand,
blonde hair spilling from her cap,
long tan thighs,
tall white sox.

She is not baseball at all,
but a harmless grace here,
a tiny joy
glimpsed one time each inning,
when she bends
and, oh God give us extra innings,
picks up the ball.

We applaud, and nature
is good.

Les humains savent tant de jeux l'amour la mourre
L'amour jeu des nombrils ou jeu de la grande oie
La mourre jeu du nombre illusoire des doigts
Seigneur faites Seigneur qu'un jour je m'énamoure

Watching the game of work,
I wonder at the big owe
how dark in my heart is the place where we all
could not make the play,
fell to earth crooked,
swung a bat too late,
threw far over the fielder's head,
cringed in fear of the hardness,
or the coach who scorned our fear.

Here is the fancied green of our wishes,
here where I still think the ballplayers are older than I,
this is where they are unreasonably adept,
where our failure is turned inside out,
by quick hands and an always-white ball.

I sit in section nine and sometimes wonder why,
but know I am at ground zero
where art is made,
                    where there is no profit,
no loss.

        The planet lies perfect in its orbit.

Diamonds,
                this green diamond at Little Mountain,
where these younger than we leap and run and fall
like our older brothers,
                                    where we shout inanities
from our high wall,
                              our wit echoes loudly
from the right-field fence.

                                       This is not
poetry,
           neither is it play;
                                       it is life
whether you like it or not,
                                         money
changes hands,
                        the sun goes purple and gold
behind the trees,
                          the lights come on bright,
the ball is white,
                         and someone
has to pay for it.

Dear spooks:
if there were a domed stadium between the stars
upon whose Astroturf athletic lovers
made plays beyond the hearts of these heroes,
daring ozone catches in deepest centre,
stolen base
in a cloud of crystal,
delightful silent hand-shakes
at home plate—

and if they could arouse the crowd
of long-ghosted millions to a standing ovation,
a thunder-clap around the park,

would that throng
cast blossoms of immortality over nine heads,
bring at last a satisfied smile to the face
between these shoulders here on earth,
on the road,
in last place?

ELEGY SIX

Yes, I see you, backyard raspberries,
you've been there
all my life,
all thru my verse.
One day you
spit white blossoms,
and when I dont immortalize them
you hang a million heavy cones,
your branches droop
to the earth with dark berries;
I cant pursue
your quickness.
The first moment out of sleep, and you
are ecstatic.
I sit in my pyjamas and read the
kitchen newspaper,
glance at your pride.
A god
could have scampered across the lawn while I was
turned to the stove, looking for coffee.

We hang on,
plugging for fame,
scotch-taping our blossoms to
our already browning stems.
When we produce
at last our final over-ripe fruit,
the earth around us
is already frozen,
the family snug abed for winter.

But we know a few who sprout flames in the dark before morning,
lighting the air we've only learned to breathe,
these godlike voices signing from their still-skinny bodies.

We make heroes of them,
jealously, we know
they are touched,
they spring the most glorious
green reeds along our rusty lanes,
they took
the beautiful back road to death.

They turn
bright circles of colour,
like the painted bicycle
wheels of Greg Curnoe,
king child.

ou bien le corps
quand il se prend
pour seul témoin
d'un avenir
impérissable

You cant catch their breath with your fingers,
heroes
are strange,
they are ghosts of the dying young,
they don't care for survival,
they rise and spread
being.
Every flower is an exploding star.
Few
have the nerve to sniff that scent,
I never
drove out of Kerrisdale into Death Valley in my
dead hero's time-bomb automobile.
I never heard
the detonation behind his blue eyes.

In twenty years I've never heard his like.
                                        But last night
the first fall wind cut the bamboo beside my window,
and his black song entered,
                                rattling the papers off my desk.

Beauty is the first prod of fear—
I would escape
this awful longing.
I want to be a kid
with all this before me,
Georgie on the rug, reading
of Jesus,
eyeing my mother,
wondering whether she knows.

Mary mother of Pearl,
he was a hero in your womb.

He began the swift race there,
he chose you for his
irritating arena.
Envy pulsed in a thousand other bellies,
as he chose a stance,
flexed and began.
His first miracle
was his escape from your dark embrace
into this awful longing.

You mothers of the bright flash,
before you can imagine,
the upstairs bedroom is empty at night,
your house
is for a moment ringed in a glow of blossoms,
stars
rain on the roof,
suicides attest to the fearsome
beauty of your issue.

You had a quick joy.

There were no witnesses,
then a million.

Each word of love
moved your son a mile,
each loving hand touched him
like the wind,

When they saw him raise his arms at the tape
he was no racer but erased;

in his pace the blinking corner of a constellation.

ELEGY SEVEN

No more love poems for you,
dear old voice,
you've outgrown them here on this street of leaves.

I know,
I know, you can still do it,
turn words
as those swallows turn quick in the air they know.

But each of them falls and is eaten,
and you
are only consumed.

Even while pretty ears listen
you rise above them,
past those handy trees, looking
for a listener who has not announced herself.

You speak a language you are only now learning,
hoping she will hear you,
knowing she is yourself
out there.

Lightning and love,
if spring were here
she would listen and nod her head,
your music
would announce her erotic shape everywhere.

First
her naked ankle,
your first words,
and then still
weak silver sun gathered round her filmy dress,
your stanzas made an everywhere.

She walks
and rises,
flowers in the sky round her hair,
blossoms her cape,
blooms where she has stepped,
your music made colour.

You swell your lungs
and invent summer,
up at earlier light, up
before the heavy trees,
spilling heat down those mountains
to ripple over the pavement of 41st Avenue,
bring
shop women to the sidewalk for air.
Others are
zipping by on bikes,
powerful thighs brown in the sun,
power everywhere,
boys crashing into third base
at Elm Park,
old geezers with gentleman shoulders
rolling heavy orbs over pressed turf,
late afternoon
meeting of hips,
bedsheets thrown into a corner.

Powerful voice,
the summer nights here, in summer
the night belongs to earth at last,
those stars
are thrown into space from earth.

We should
go among them,
learn them all,
know especially
the roads between them.

We should never forget them.

They are made from dead poets' voices.

I've called,
I've sung to a lover,
but when she appeared
she brought with her a team of womanly figures,
shapes risen from remembered graves.

One's voice
belongs to them all,
they all want to rise to earth again.

Dear children to come,
remember this word above all else:
what you live all your life to be,
you are now.

You will scamper after your love,
win the race,
and run smiling,
your chest heaving,
where you are now,
before freedom,
in the open.

Where you are now.
It is lovely to be here.
Even you know that,
you women lost in your familiar
dirty coats in front of a broken door,
a pissy hotel
on East Hastings,
rain on passing cop cars, somewhere
you know it.
For each of you there was an hour,
There was a long minute,
a time I can measure
with half a line,
when your eyes were wide enough
for your soul to leap out,
stand and say

yes,
here I am,
I am.
Entire.
You felt it beating
against your nerve-ends.

But you and I do forget
what the people across the lawn can never see,
what they may never desire of us.
No, we have to
turn it outside,
we want everyone to see it, we
forget the lovely world we have been dying to see
is still inside;
we have to transform it
in the open,
inside.

Dans l'onde toi devenue
Ta jubilation nue.

Corny, isn't it?
                    The world turns within us,
while we transform it,
                              fancy words but true,
sweetheart.

                 The alleged world outside fades before our eyes.

Remember that big house at 38th and Larch?
Look now:
                A translucent spectre rises there,
                                                  comfortable
as the notion of home still building in your brain.

So all your neighbours have built this city block,
ethereal as their own passing conversations.

                                              They
would put leaves on their naked pear trees.

They build a stadium of the heart downtown,
and will never find their way to the game.

But you and I,
                                  as they say,
                                                              you and I will keep our hearts'
architecture in secret;

                                                  if one structure deserved praise,
if once it was turned to with humble love,
we preserve it where it will never be razed, in-
visible.

                Nearly everyone walks by it as the eye
past a dark star,
                                    poor sad bozos, their hearts
empty,
                finding no familiar temple to bow down to
and imagine,
                             inside where the outside is.

Poor sad *insensati,*
                I see them in Kerrisdale and Trieste;

each time our heavy earth turns its outside to the dark sky,
it carries idiots who have given up the past
and lost the future.

                Poor men,
                        even tomorrow is beyond sight.

But you and I don't have to discard our eyes, our
open eyes preserve the form we still recognize.

This, This, This
                stood in the city's heart,
                                stood
in the storm of chance,
                it stood there
while the streets evaporated,
                        it stood where
light from a million stars converged.

I'll show it to you,
it's there now,
we took it down
brick by brick and rebuilt it here,
we build it every day,
I'll take you there,
it's here where you
have eyes to see.

Look up,
if you can imagine, up
there,
the light on the roof above that darkened town.

How's that for "glistening with creation"?

Isnt that
a wonder?
Human expression, human desire.

Go back to the stars
and tell them about that,
tell them in your language,
I'm out of breath,
I couldn't begin ...

Tell them
we're not dead yet,
not while we honour the space inside,
rebuild the luminous palace there.

Palace?
The gymnasium
of our veins.

It must be enormous.
After five thousand years
there is rooming room on the floor.

That shining roof,
you must see it from your abode,
you must be able to look thru the top windows.

Our songs must reach your highway between the stars.

But that young woman,
staggering with love
from the parked car to her door—
I think her hair
has to brush across your leg.

But no more love songs for you,
I said,
you wouldnt listen anyway,
would you?

My song says I'm holding you
off,
remember?

That hand I hold toward you
is not open,
it is a fist under your nose,
I'm not one with you yet.

I'll stay here awhile,
go to lunch in Kerrisdale,
wonder what edifice
can glow within the hurried waitress.

ELEGY EIGHT

for Michael Ondaatje

Today I saw two robins feeding on worms along Yew Street,
eyes wide,
                    looking into the open air, they
were not beset by past and future and wishfulness.

All animals see with their eyes what is before them.

But we look elsewhere,
                                        our eyes bind things
to our desires,
                         our fears mock the great trees
in this neighbourhood.

                                        Oh oh, says the anxious reviewer,
this poet is not in control of his materials.

Only by watching the birds fly do we know
there is sky between the trees.

I force my daughter
to learn the names of the continents, names
that snare the past.
That's how we stay living
over centuries.

The robin sees me coming,
his act
is not fear,
he moves only to keep his eye on me.

He will eat and fly and die,
and reach eternity
without naming it.

We dissolve into hungers,
our breath disappears every minute,
we can measure
our remaining store with a hand-held calculator.

Not for a day do we live only in space,
where windflowers open without history.
We live on a wheel,
never in Śūnyatā, where the lungs rest
un-numbered.

I see my daughter's body come to rest,
her eyes set somewhere I envy,
and like a miserly Latin master,
I wave my fingers before her face.
I'm afraid
she's visiting the domain of not-being,
not-bothering-to-be,
damn it, what a coward.
To sneer at the meditating cat,
to avoid the face
of the nearly dead,
who looks like an animal in peace.

We remember getting there while making love,
                                                                        nearly
to losing all care,
                        to the open,
                                        where all that matters
falls away, nearly.
                        Where the only other body
keeps us here.

                    We come back finally
to looking at the watch on the familiar wrist,
reaching for the cigarette,
                                horizontal clichés,
                                                        remembering
where the underwear is,
                            moving an awkward elbow
that keeps us from being nowhere.

                                        The open had been
just beyond her,
                        but you were in her, she
is after all,
                the world.

As I walk past the hedges of Kerrisdale all I see
is a translation of the open,
                                             nature to our advantage
pressed,
               or the natural eye of a robin
looking past me to the sky.

                                             Stupid fate,
to be nothing more than this,
                                                 a foreign timetable,
an unwanted designer trampling the woods.

Des forces que tu tiens ta liberté dispose,
Mais de tous tes conseils l'univers est absent.

If this hairy dog trotting down Yew Street
knew what I know,
he'd get my ass in his teeth
and never let go.
But he knows what his nose does,
And sees the first few feet of eternity.

I know
the fiction of my past and expect to walk
straight into my fancied future.

He walks,
we see indulgently,
on an angle,
from bush to bush;
when we see a busy dog walk straight and quick,
we say how like a man.

Dog and robin,
we made no streets for you.

Yet look again at the dog's hanging head,
                                        a weight
we think we know lies on his neck.

                                        All memories
are sad,
        he has them too,
                        is this true?

                                        We look
with whipped expectation for something
we used to curl up in,
                        turn in circles three times
and lie down.

            It was tender.
                        We slept. Without
open eye we nuzzled and there we were.

                                        Here
we have to run to reach,
                        but do we reach?

There—remember?—it was enough to breathe.
                                            Home
was next to a loud heart.
                        Now we are in the street
too long for our feet.

Ah, those lucky little beings who never leave mother,
burrow in a womb that is world.
These curled
insects that live under the tatters of my gladioli,
fetal,
knowing all they touch was there
when they were born.

That happy robin again,
seems to know,
he may bounce or fly,
in a matrix
that includes the sky.

He does not know he is
the image of a pedestrian heart,
come from
a belly near another heart,
here to chatter between trees,
tipping wing,
skidding across his own wakened air,
like a pen across a modern poem.

Let us go then,
                              heart and eye,
                                                        to look as always,
attend as always,
                                look at the world and never
out of it.

                   It begins to fall down a little.
We renovate and proudly show our friends.

Cracks appear, and we patch them.
                                                                  Cracks appear in us
and our friends appear to watch.
                                                            To be
watching.

                    Dogs walk by;
                                             birds fly, away.

Why do I keep getting lost this way,
                                        four blocks
from home,
          or is it a city away?
                                    I get turned around,
no matter what street I take,
                                  so I always look
like a man saying goodbye.

                                 Like a banished citizen
allowed one last look at Kerrisdale,
                                       yellow leaves
falling on lawns,
             I hesitate,
                                 trying to remember it all,
every day the same farewell.

Goodbye, warm world
who gave me birth
and told me
not to stick around.

ELEGY NINE

The laurel bush grows enormous, nearly obliterating
the front steps and pouring its dark waxy leaves over
into the porch.

I never sit there, though I could,
there are two Yankee Stadium seats on the porch.

I could sit there,
reading poetry,
imitating
that robust companion,
reading, perhaps, Mallarmé.

But
they said I had to be
human,
running from doom,
longing for fortune.

Half the beautiful ones I have known are gone.

My longing is not for happiness—
that only proves

your days are leaving one by one.

Not even to see
what's in the mail this morning.

Not just
to get the sap running,
any bush can do that.

Because here this once I can be bound to
meaning,
                because it looks as if the world wanted me,
the disappearing neighbourhood needs my step.

I will be the first to go,
                                    my one chance spent so quick.

One for you, too.
                            One chance to offer to the world
meaning.

                No second stanza to develop,
                                                you'd better
write a good first verse.

                                    But you could have
died in the womb,
                            you did get this one blank page.

No eraser can undo your visit.

On my dresser upstairs you'll find a limestone pebble
I brought across the sky from a cliffside path
at Duino.

                I'll leave it here when I go,
                                                    along with
everything else.

                          Just so,
                                       we run over earth,
carry pieces of it in our hands,
                                                so we squeeze it
and demand meaning,
                                     we urge it to resemble our heart.

I brought eleven pieces of Duino home with me
and gave away ten,
                               but think the one I retain
is really me,
                    I haven't given away anything.

I want to keep it in my bedroom forever.

Importun
Vent qui rage!
Les défunts?
Ça voyage.

Our words will stay—maybe—pebbles to tell of our pain,
the hard path we had to walk for a few years,
the long long moments of love,
                                                            or trying to love.

Things that could never be told,
                                                            so we gave words instead.

Stranger yet the nights we got out from under the street lamps,
could see the still,
                                    stars at least,
                                                            feel
a little homesick.

                                    Then we knew enough to come back empty.

No one brings a stone away from that home.

I came back in the morning,
                                        eyes half open,
                                                                to say
chestnut tree, laurel bush, cherry, front porch, eyes
open,
        to tell bird, window, lover, determined insect
happily burrowed in the earth round these gladioli.

To count them and bind them to life,
                                                    to praise
them and energize the earth.

                                        Those lovers in the car
are seduced not by each other but by secret earth
filled with proper desire for transfiguration.

                                                                That I
should say such a word in a poem.

                                                They kiss
and feel the press of more than their own flesh, they are happy
to add their hot hands
to the never-ending shaping and praising of the world.

The trick of the dance is in following,
now the words,
allegro,
          now the contrary beat of the glossy leaf.

It is time to speak now,
                                        to say the words that are
ready,
            to name the world we can still see,
                                                                        the leaves
depart their tree but the tree is here.

                                                              Speak, praise,
before the tree is gone with your going,
                                                                    before
you become act without words.

                                                      It is no bed of roses,
being dead.
                    Your silent blood is a message
from a dying messenger.
                                          It is filled with words
your tongue can move into sound,
                                                            words your neighbourhood
deserves.

The ghastly dead will never applaud your imitation of them,
your beautiful silence.

They wrote the book on silence.

They own the rights to invisible meaning.

Show them
something made of earth,
bring out the footstool
your father made in high school shop,
a necklace
your grandmother bought from a Haida fisherman;

things,
made by hands and real as their names.

Say look at these marvels,
we did these, we
have eyes and hands,
our best poet said
the optic heart must venture.

They will stare
and applaud,
as you did,
watching
the father and son on Querétaro Street bending cane
to make chairs till the light fell up the walls.

Praise our things.

                                        They are innocent in our hands,
the sweet pain of Archie Shepp's tenor saxophone
lives for fingers and ears,
                                                        show them how we love,
how we grace the earth a horn is fashioned from.

The earth,
                        how it requires us to live,
                                                                    how it
desires to become us.

                                                How the ash trees along Larch Street
turn to me for their life,
                                                    to this ephemeron in running shoes.

All right,
I hear you,
I know you want to grow again
in another soil,
if that's what I am.
To disappear
and live again in me.
All your seasons have been
practice transformations.
Is this possible?
Am I
going mad in Kerrisdale?
Lightning and love,
if spring comes again she will nod her head
in my heart—
all right, I agree,
you may die
and move in.
I will give you a new name.

Another mouth to feed,
what's that?
I was a child,
God knows what I'll be tomorrow.
Now I'm a new
husband,
now I am something like two.

ELEGY TEN

Est-ce toi, Nomade, qui nous passera ce soir aux
rives du réel?

If I endure, when this ghastly truth has passed my eyes,
may I raise music to my dead family in the dark.

Lift this light horn and play a song I know but
have never learned,
                    fingers touching keys I cannot see
through tears I always knew were there.

                                        Remember
when we were kids,
                    how we wept and secretly
loved our tears?

                How wise we were,
                                    children see
where they are going.
                    How their parents and teachers
mock them,
            drilling, memorizing happy little songs.

In November the wind slides in from the sea
and eats at our faces.

We should smile and bow,
it is the air of a sweet and terrible quartet.

Precious
agony.

How we threw away half our lives
waiting like cows for better weather.

Suffering
is our winter of bare branches,

our secret abode.

So we walk like strangers in Kerrisdale streets,
feet sore in our shoes,
forehead aching from our
squint in the rain.

The slapping of car tires on wet street
resounds from walls and fences,
engines droning
on the next block,
noise folding into noise till
we hear nothing but the occasional climbing DC-10.

We are inside an enormous overturned empty cup.

The shingled Anglican church across 37th Avenue,
highrises filled with perfumed widows asleep,
cosy women's-wear shoppes on 41st,
all
could be flattened by one ghost stepping off
the road between the stars.

But all winter the parks will be green,
and in the parks
the shades of kids and dads,
running from base to base,
throwing balls,
falling over dogs,
dutifully dropping
ice-cream wrappers in trash barrels,
a lot of
shouting under trees filled with shades of leaves.

(And across the field,
real-estate plotters wondering
who to bribe,
to grab all that green and call it
undeveloped.)

Later in the bars on Hastings Street
dads and others down that lovely gold stuff,
get gold
into their veins,
find something to laugh about,
avoid
falling chairs,
and convince themselves they'll never die.

They'll get into a car in two o'clock rain but never die.
There's a traffic cop called Real Death but he's
on the other side of town,
where strangers are assholes.

In the after-hours joint full of smoke children are playing guitars,
lovers are propped against their clothes,
the toilet flushes endlessly behind the thin wall.

A slightly drunk dad is amazed by the different beauty
of a thin young woman with sorrow in her eyes.

It takes a while to determine that she's here alone,
she doesnt have a car,
her thin shoulders implore, they
demand to be nuzzled.
She's too good for this place.

With a stupid remark he begins a conversation
whose intention is to find out whether he can afford
to take her home.

Even when she says she lives
on the road between the stars,
he finds cause
to think she's lovely.
But he also thinks that he
is stupid.

He buys another tequila screwdriver
and drifts,
and drives home to early morning Kerrisdale,
his windshield wipers crossing the wet snow in her eyes.

Like an old singing branch I call out,
                                                                    but only
those who died in their first cantos follow her home.

Dying girls and dying boys,
                                                  they follow her home.

Girls envy her rich diaphanous comet-tail dress,
boys hold her sweet cold hand,
                                                        walking from her car.

They are at last near the abode where the immortals are
all as beautiful as she,
                                          the ghastly company,
                                                                          refusing
a closing couplet.

All as beautiful,
and all with sorrowful eyes;

one
more proximate than the rest converses with the young visitor,
the newly dead.

We were all strong like you,
she says,
all like you fit to be praised.

We made this place by our coming here,
we worked
with what was left.
We drew from our own eyes
the molecules laid on one another for this city.

She signalled to some others who joined them
as they walked about the streets.

                                                            Look, she said,
at the tall apartments held aloft by faint sighs
drifting from the mouths of lorn pensioners in their rooms.

She gestured to the tall trees,
                                                    their brilliant limbs
fashioned from tears,
                                        the bordering flowers grown only
out of pain.

                    Every back yard is prowled by cats
with eyes of sharp grief,
                                            fixed on birds
that fill the trees and rooftops with songs of their agony.

Only in a shaded chamber of his stilled mind
does this youth realize he has been strolling through Kerrisdale
                and around the earth.

He does not recognize me as he passes with his escort,
nor do I see him.

                          Only the breeze fails in saying
what it half wants me to hear,
                                        on the shores of the real.

When light slips up the walls and away,
                                                    they lead him
to the graveyard on 41st Avenue,
                                              eerie tautology
in a neighbourhood of unseen grannies,
                                                    glistening
with decreation.

                        And as all the light races skywards
to settle as tight calligraphy on the black dome above,
they walk with him to the school ground on the hill
and bid him read.

                         He sees,
                                      it is an unfolded road map,
ghastly brother to the grid he's made of his life in secret,
a call to greater travel,
                              a total denial of abode.

When he lifts his eyes to look there,
                                                he knows
he is truly gone.

A new ghost,
                    his half-wrinkled brain out of sync,
he cannot see the neighbourhood clear.

                                                        But she
tells the narrative of the newly dead to its hero—

a black bird in the dark night descends like the last leaf
from the chestnut tree outside his unseen house,
past his open unseeing eyes,
                                        past his alert ear,
offering a song where no bird sings at night on earth,
a short poem of unwelcome comfort,
                                                    a direction
to read where reading erases the words
line by line,
                 street by street.

Till the last page opens onto the earth
beyond his darkened acres,
                                                  above invisible branches.

Every star becomes a coal as he reads it,
                                                                      figures
turning to ashes:
                              the Archer, the Scribe,
the one he's always called the Infielder, to the south
the Triestino,
                         quickly followed by the Coyote,
the Wine Glass, Erato, the three-armed Saguaro.

Last to go,
                     drawing his reluctant gaze,
the clear white diamonds of the Number Nine.

Love is yearning for the stars,
they will
come on again inside the committed dead.

Time falls from him
as he follows his vaporous guides as far as they may go.

You have walked along this street,
their beautiful leader tells him
most of your life,
you recognize that dark doorway,
and that.

In the morning the shopkeepers
will not see you
but feel your presence in the wind,
make satisfied jests about the season's immediate cold.

She looks at him a last time with her lorn eyes
and he is alone.

He walks out of Kerrisdale a last time,
                                        not turning to look
but seeing it all.

                    The sun rises unknown to him.

His feet no longer feel the pavement.

                                        If he did cry out,
none would hear.

But as he goes,
his going lifts our eyes;
we see
a little more from time to time.

November sun
on the maple's cushioning moss,
bamboo canes
across the corner of a window,
he leaves us this;

we rush to call it meaning.

We see everything's entry,
the robins that sing,
la la,
the muscular dog that trots down our street the first time,

each quick appearance is a farewell.

The single events that raise our eyes and stop our time
are saying goodbye, lover,
goodbye.

Irritable Reaching

Vancouver
1984

(Coach House, 1986)

With thanks to Audrey Thomas

who gave me the little notebook

this was written in

MIRRORS SHOW

Mirrors show up empty, windows turn black,
and mannequins stand in couples back to back;
ripples rise in ponds unbidden by the wind,
giving old misgivings to a maiden who has sinned
against a godlike apparition dressed in green and
red and acting unimagined where mannequins stand,
each meaning something to this watcher but nought
to one another, only to their fiction wrought.

Always they will gesture in the attitudes arrested,
totally dependent on the climate of her heart,
wholly in the power of a dreamer interested
only in the reasons they are fixedly apart;
only when they're naked and their plastic torsos nested
does the watcher think their fiction has its start.

COOL STREETS

Cool streets sound like home now, insects
leave him alone to worry himself, his face
always a surface acted upon. The swampy south
recedes as he writes it out, as he wrecks,
kills, disembowels the body of that other place.

Body that disappears under layers of reports,
layers of pain described, consigned to out past;
alive in this new old land, he cheers the cold
itself. He fancies his beginning as a sport
star, an import eyeing a home field at last,
even as his aching body tells him he's getting old.

VALOUR CALLS

Valour calls a man to place
in darkest lair his shaven face;
county meals will give him beard
to best the animal he feared,
or would his tongue expand a tale
raucous as a nightingale.

Cooks and barbers ever vie
over souls of those who die;
lovers ever dine and shave,
enter parlour, enter cave;
men who will not venture there
always finish in the air,
never satisfied, nor care.

FALLING THRU

Falling thru a medium that holds
right to the bottom of our world's bottom,
all those decks, those married, those holds,
never longer heard are seen at bottom,
killed by salt, seen by him who sees—

Diving into Jonesy's silted locker
after depth where sunshafts do not go
very like the eyes that search a locker
ever after swimmers will not go,
yet doomed to vision, being he who sees.

MAN OR BEAST

Man or beast is not
all times a choice;
right or wrong a voice
inside a city;
animals may love you into thought,
never pity.

Every brute sports a tongue declaring
need, but is it his or your uncaring
greed that speaks—
even in the forest greed speaks—
leaving the city to thought, greed speaks.

BRAIN THAT VANISHES

Brain that vanishes among its traces,
running before a cool-eyed pursuit,
is seen every time that finger races
across a canvas, a canvas across
near seas, wet lines, a deck man's boot.

For lines are there to hold something
i cannot perceive at their ends;
seeing the lines is to hold something
however the rest of me bends;
eyes are instructed to hold something
resting where so much depends.

JUST AS WE LOSE

Just as we lose the last of innocence
one comes to tell us there's more;
her date of birth is unimaginable,
no one has seen her before.

Goodness and mercy are such temptations,
love is a bear in the street;
all our old friends are resting their angers,
shuffling their cards and their feet,
shuffling their hands and their feet—
calling off war with the last of our innocence
one swaggers down to defeat.

PHONES RING OUT

Phones ring out in open air,
ears attend what isnt there,
totally dependent on the climate of his heart;
echoes linger everywhere
ringing thru the static where they never thought to
start.

He moves elusively, never standing
uselessly, that silent aging;
soothingly he steps, demanding
earnest music of our raging.

TAKING INK

Taking ink from his heart,
ink for his art,
mister print was designed from the start.

Itself he fancies, his beginning
never doubted. He faces fate's
kiss, a touch, an impressing
set of stets   he hesitates
to name. He marks an echoing
ear, he steps upon a plate
right beneath the life he's etching.

GRACE REQUIRES AGE

Grace requires age in this diffident land—
every brute sports a tongue, but few may speak
or taste a decent vintage from Thalia's hand;
raucous poetasters broadcast every week,
grating our cliffs of language into sand,
eradicating the inheritance of the meek.

Just five old men are shaping all our grace:
one wears beard of white upon his face;
high above the northern sea he cruises
northward for the silver fish he chooses,
soaring on inconstant swells of air,
then knifes into the salt and spears a pair
of lines no other eyes have ever found
nor ears had grace and sea enough to sound.

READY TO SNAP

Ready to snap, he focuses
on infinity, holds his finger,
yes, holds his nerve, gives a

Kiss to the quick singer
in your ear. He's recorded
your soul. He's painted your face
on silver. Shine back
on his open eye your instant grave,
kiss him in a glace,
as his wide eye to dance.

DETACHMENT FROM SELF

Detachment from self is authentic love
even in autobiographical times;
need (but is it his or your uncaring
nerves him to scribe his acts from above?)
inches him toward confession and crimes,
sometimes called order, sometimes overbearing.

Losing that self is not simply to shove
ego aside while composing honest lines;
even loss of ego is a mantle for the wearing.

RELIEF OCCURS

Relief occurs above the surface,
over planes of handled black;
names of something pretty nervous

Mean a nothing further back—
art is more than just a smear
regardless of the youngster's knack;
thank the lord he is not here
in my world of coloured service,
neither here nor there, nor here.

COOL STREETS SOUND

Cool streets sound like home now, insects

Just self-absorbed neighbours, perplex.

Never look a donor in the face,
even when he isnt of your race;
white anglo saxon pennies roll,
making dollars scurry down their hole;
always begging near your father's store,
no one's ever seen you here before.

TEARING OFF THE SHROUDS

Tearing off the shrouds of night,
over plains of handled white,
never letting shadows lie,
yet he demonstrates his eye.

Only curvature is there,
now a single, now a pair;
less is more and least is life,
even loss is loss of life—
yet he demonstrates his eye.

BONES ALONG HER BODY

Bones along her body show
art is never far below,
reason offers equal space
bones that glimmer in her face;
art is never far from where
reason offers up its chair—
art is never far away.

Phones ring out in open air,
ears deduce a message there,
noises all fall into place,
tones that need no special grace;
letting half her reason go,
art is never far from so,
never far when she will play
dancing bones on reason's day.

PRESS IT PERFECT

Press it perfect
every time,
take it to the
edge of rime,
run it out as

Quick as ink,
up and down
and like a wink;
reason offers
twenty hours
every day that
rime will flower—
mister print
and mistress mint
in perfection
never stint.

GROUND AND SKY

Ground and sky, water and leaf
or eyes that see them there
ready at the mind's wink
drop in moments into a frame
or rise a man's height, till
now they stand, taking his place.

Rime will flower with belief
and eyes will call it fair,
yet in time will also blink—
nothing lasts forever, fame
or love deferred will pass, still
reason making mulch of grace.

JUST FIVE

Just five old men are shaping all our graces
and living known to few upon the land;
churls of our time dont see their faces,
knowing neither art nor artist's hand.

Some fall into our favour only once;
he shakes the country's spirit every year,
and then few know of our deliverance
denied the eyes of reason or of fear;
but working close to heaven he persists,
on matter made of earth his finger races;
little do the dolts care of his fists
that rime our pummelled earth with heaven's graces.

MONSIEUR HAS MADE

Monsieur has made a country out of *femmes*
in which their love of laughter is a right;
cold hands and burning souls embrace their men,
hard hands and melting hearts their nation's might;
elections will be held when every *homme*
learns how to love his reason like his mom.

Tones that need no special grace are his,
rimes that rise out of that place are meet,
every citizen who meets him is
made a little freer on his feet;
but reason tells him freedom can away
like clapping hands that end the final act—
a maker needs to make another play,
yet lets his *femmes* turn fancy into fact.

THE EYE IN HIDING

The eye in hiding lies
or lets us see his trace,
nor shows us all his face,
yet demonstrates or dies.

Unless we learn his rimes
reason runs away,
quiet dulls the day,
unless we read our times;
he moves across our lives
and colours all our ways,
regards with hidden gaze
the "we" which he contrives.

JUST AS WE LOSE AT LAST

Just as we lose at last
our resistance to disco,
news comes singing from

Vienna, San Francisco,
incredible New York,
Chicago and Bayreuth;
knowledge precedes taste
even in Detroit,
reason tells us crime will follow loss of rime,
Samson shows us heart will follow rise of art.

PASTORAL MUSIC

Pastoral music seems like home now,
home now far from reason's door;
yesterday's music sounds like Rome now,
long ago and long before;
listening ears can hear a poem now
in the steps on forest floor
saying softly evermore.

Walls do not fall here,
echoes do not stay
behind the phantom walls here
beauty comes to play.

HE SAID

He said face that problem
or side-step it
when you come to it.

Taking ink from his heart,
on his open eye he laid it.

Drive, he advised,
or park the car, he said.

I see no rime, no reason,
time nor season.

DANCING BONES

Dancing bones on reason's day,
artful frame of reference,
very nearly 'scape the eye
in rimes that leap the outer fence,
dodging realists on their way.

Young in flesh and young in ear,
older than this land in wit,
under walls he passes by
napping old thematic crit,
garrison of lazy fear.

ZEAL IN THE DEFENCE

Zeal in the defence against liberty
opens the eyes of the eyes of rime,
names the secret names of things,
kills the murderers of time,
opening locks, closing the box.

Delayed Mercy

Vancouver
August 21, 1984–December 22, 1984

(Coach House, 1987)

I live by day

Full of faith and courage

And perish by night

In holy fire.

—Novalis

I

A PENDULOUS LIP

fr Tom Raworth

Bodies held shaped by the pressure of air,
the pleasure of hair, for her a ball
in the stomach.

We smile at her, cigarettes
burning the paint on the window sill
where we sit still, a cat
in our eyes, her name

Iris.

        She cuts us to pieces every time
she walks across the linoleum.
A Chinese territory we werent there
to name.

Cancer bundles up & prepares to emerge
with colours that'll astound us;
we wait like a committee, our teacher
hacking behind us.

                                Cuban volunteers
cut cane & we dont even
dream about them. Planes take off
on time, our shoes find each other
in the dark. Bodies dont.

OPEN BIOLOGY

fr Tom Clark

Just as the dependable horizon of a fence
calms the eye, so a slot inside the brain
seeks its permanence. A limit set
on novelty.

                    The cat broods in his room,
prisoner of our self dis-regard. If we
could walk like him, coal would slither
down a chute.

Do you remember coal falling? The dust
seeks a level inside your lung
where song belongs.

                                   Over the fence,
a homer brooding inside our hope,
the green field under the lights
they want to deny me. Do you remember
coal falling? Drop coal
all over that meadow.

A lonely man is pacing there, reciting
songs to himself, history of inside,
shared feline surety.

Did you call, & did anyone answer?
Did a ball whizz by your head?

PEN IN HAND, BEARD ON HEAD

fr Ed Sanders

I say, let them open up
a million files on us. Be like the cat
under the porch, ever vigilant, suspicious
& fiercely confident.

Take time to dance,
a King Sunny Adé in white shining silk,
in front of thumping here they go drums,
and, uh uh, talking
flowers when the lights go on under the roof,

it must be dark somewhere, dish eyes
reflect any thought opened their direction.

A blue hat, cover of a book, tipped,
opened, read what's inside, a brain
made of words.

Take time to dance, no cat in that hat, only
a greyhound in the moonlight, escape
from the medicine line of suspicion.

Let them open up
a million brains, step back, wet
Tuesday night all over
their matching black suits.

THE SINK'S LEAKING

fr David McFadden

Like radio signals from frantic planets
your thoughts seek a place in the world,
your thoughts & mine. What am I
thinking of right now, Paul Newman
looking like a father.

                                        An orange cat
held in the arms over the shoulder
of a woman growing steadily
more beautiful.

Cats dont think, their expressionless faces
turn from side to side, feral machines
like heartbeats going forever.

                                                        That's how short
the temper is, that's how hard the steel is,
the mind trying to get my attention right now.

Like radio signals from frantic planets
everything comes to an end, you say.
Did you ever see dirt on the ground
come to an end? Thought is dirt.

Signals are illusions, cats pretend
they can see them. They cant see anything
but food, shit, water, furniture. They
are simply lucky enough to make people think
they're beautiful.

AFTER THE DANCE

fr Ron Loewinsohn

A radiant pudgy lady
at a wedding where she knows hardly anyone,
that's my heart.

What did you expect,
a shard of steel, a hard glance
from a man in a tree?

Aspens
hardly tremble as I do, they with no weight
but the wind in them.

Rented clouds disperse showers on this terrain,
horsemen seek shelter where they can,
words slip down the new streams,
leaving messages on the banks
no one can read.

What did you expect, a cat's smile
in the branches? Cats write
the worst poems in the language.
I remain dull & satisfied with prose
fetched up with the compost.

You want a figure more fresh than that?
Then bring it up from your own heart,
bring the worms, dont let them fall off the hulk,

bring a gleaming sail boat.

A CAMERA SITTING IDLE

fr Christopher Dewdney

The forest is filled with eyes, clear
unblinking surprises—

Thought I saw a long falling star,
but it was a moth descending
the shaft of lamp light. White shiny silk
an intelligence
I reach for, long to possess.

What a liar, the intelligence that lives
here in me, I'm glad of, dont know
what planet it came from,

yearns for the stars if they're there;
if they're not, play ball against Duthie Books.

Watching a moth fall is reading. Reading
emerged ahead of writing, & both
before speech.
                                        There is a lot of very old stuff
to be speechless before.
& after.

There's no real forest around here, only
captive trees, eyes & branches,
retinae looking out between the bars.

A MASK OVER THE EYES

fr Stephen Rodefer

Build a wall around the self & dont go
in. Stay outside in the cold night air,
of any story's beginning, where
you've thrown the cats.

It is dark,
finally, everywhere, the centre of the outside
is dark, black as a mother's imagination.

Build a wall around the self & dont go in.
Did you think you'd win an award
for self-abnegation? Forget it, forget
long blonde hair rippling in the wind,
oiled skin rippling over flext muscles,
forget the white Hawai'ian beach,
it is dark now as a human thought.

Build a wall around the self & dont go in.
Did you plan all your life to remain young
when you grew old? Persuade yourself to forget.

Your life is rippling under the skein of water
called public attention, someone puts in a toe
& you're gone.

Stay there, wherever you are,
outside my self too. The noise of steel on steel
is all the poetry I need, that
& half a glass or saucer of cold milk
to get all the cigarettes out of my throat.

II

FRENCH SOMETHING IN THE OVEN

fr Ted Berrigan

So the old fat flies toward the brain
we were born with. Pardon me, is that
the editorial we?

No editors here, chum,
only blue birds invisible against a blue sky,
mirrors on their wings for your blue eyes.

Old fat birds are an omen of death, oh
it may take years but it's on the road,
& you are a roadside inn.

These pronouns are confusing & so personal,
I can eye birds in the sky & fat,
well, maybe not fat flying toward the brain.

Tell me, if you can, old fat, what's the difference
between the brain & the blue sky? Is it
that the brain will never cloud up & rain?

Ask your editor, isnt he staying also at the inn?
Or do editors stay forever
living off the fat of the land?

Nice thing about this brain. I might lose it
before I die.

DOWN IN THE TREES

fr Tom Clark

Rays expanding from coffins
converge on you & me, it is a message
from some other planet. Death there
is life here, you should come here
where we are terrified by the approach of life.

The coffins floated out to sea
when the earth gave way, grandma's bones
tried one breastbone stroke, then sank
past the placid eyes of pink salmon.

No fat on those folks, they did their time,
found no rest, now float west
under the sea.

                         A watery grave is my heart,
dont lie there, rays pass thru
if you stand still. If you're still standing
a minute later you're alive here, dead
there.

            Let's go there, let's see
what kind of clothes they wear, what
house-pets they keep. Let's see whether
they can lie to us, straight-faced.

NOT AN EQUINOX

fr Tom Raworth

Passing time with cats
                                        is not good for the brain,
not good for the country
                                            you were going to save.

These pronouns, they should have been prepositions.
C'est le wrong time in life to be unsure
of the future, cloudy about the past, to
sit on the porch & count the seconds
you've been doing that.

                                          The first
was sometimes the best, sometimes the worst.
This is my first life, Shirley,
when "the poem" ends I die. We always
say "the poem" in quotation marks,
sometimes invisible; it is a way
of disclaiming parenthood. "The boy"
would do as well. When "the boy" is over
I die. So I will write "the boy"
for as long as I can.
                                    Kids come & go,
I call them all "the boy."

There he is now, with his ever-present cat.
A real pair, them two.

GROSS HERBS

fr Novalis

In dew drops I'll sink
                    and mix with the ashes
while "the boy" plays Scrabble for dollars.

I grit my teeth when I think of cats
walking slowly across my grave.

                                        On the Isle of Wight
Anselm's cat curled & slept
on the grave of Lord Tennyson.

                                        No rest
for the wicket, you could have bowled me over
with a pronoun. Late night poems
and children should be in bed.
                                        Flowers
closed till dawn, if we ever have dawn.

Till then a thought hurrying home
to some planet we havent learned to name
might brush by me in my own dark yard,
leap up on the fence & consider me
an intruder. If I were in a window
I would throw a clock at him.

I'll tell my father on you
he might reply.

A SWING IN THE RAIN

fr Clayton Eshleman

A caterpillar suffers in the sun,
poor little blind cat, looking for a leaf.
Put a thousand caterpillars together,
you have my brain, now there's
a pronoun we can trust.

                                        The lamp
burns down on good white paper made
of forgetfulness.

                              You see that creature
waiting in the dull light for the 17 bus?
That is the hope of your age, that is bread
going stale tomorrow.

Insects should not be fat & juicy, brains
should not be pink slime, they are hard
metal pushed against someone's hairy stomach.

                    Written children will not forgive us,
they face a tendentious life, waiting.

Oftentimes shit resembles brains, curled
hairless caterpillars, shy of scrutiny.

There are women who will kill you
for a brain, there are teachers
who will beg you not to look at them.

BROWN SOCKS IN BED

fr Brian Fawcett

Just language & a vague melody
is all I've got, these years
I've bent my body & brain to learning.

Just enough language to buy bread & jam,
keep the crust on, nourish the organs,
keep the organs in good working order
for a predator.

                                        Unjust language
in all the magazines, in the speeches
of inferior writers called government, dogs
my days, destroys my nights, calls
my imagination, home.

Strangers build concrete walls in my yard,
I pull the curtains

                                                  over my heart. They
get two hundred dollars an hour, the cats
keep off the wet cement, the one time
they could have been useful to my spite.

                    Those men will get none of my melody,
I wont even say hello to them. They know
there's a dragon inside the house, hope
he hasnt got a shotgun.

He hasnt got a shotgun, just bad language.

III

LATE ROMANTIC BROOM

fr Sharon Thesen

Small wonders collapsing just because
it's September. Such simple obedience,
why did the poets praise nature?

A poet pitied a flower up too soon,
wrong emotion, give it a smile, a new
car, shower material rewards on it.

    I want to kick blossoms wilting
when they're told to, books used to
do that well we got smart, forgot God
's wars.

            A long female neck, now there's
something the gods of nature never
thought of. We did it, it's called style.
We've got it.

                    Show me a quince that doesnt
mince. I'll show you a hero in his
prime, picking & eating, thinking
of that neck.

                    A new car with a sun roof,
& dare it to rain. Dare it to be
a "Canadian winter." If a faded house-
wife on a prairie porch sighs
for her long gone piano, knock her off
with one blast of your oily steel shotgun.

HARDWARE DISGUISE

fr Tom Clark

The organism will not be pardoned,
true enough. You thought when you were four
you'd be the first boy who didnt die,
thought maybe they'd discover perpetual life
just in time.

                    Now you try other things,
denial gone, creation, it's called. You try
creation. All right, creation only works
a little while. You try amazement. The organism
will not be pardoned.

    Amazement is a car that works
better than a flower. Amazement
is too good for them,
but chocolate in bed for you.

Sure, in dew drops I'll sink,
but dew drops never saw anything
before we came along. Never saw pronouns
free in our hands.

                            Tick tick says the clock,
& we made it do that.

See her get out of that long low car
& stretch her high legs? Nature
never made anything so beautiful, nature
is all incest.

The rose knows nothing,
                              not even pain.

GLYCERINE TRAVEL

fr Helen Adam

My bed is thorny when I lie down.
Sure, nature, I say, I allow
you'll prevail in the end, all revolutions
come at last to your suppuration.

    But I'm sleepy when I say that,
long cars drive silently by my window
in my drowse.
    On the radio they announce
childbirth, got me again. I'm about ready
to give up, invention
is for fools & dreamers, good night.

   You got me, lady, hang me high,
call the flowers to sell souvenirs,
feed the masses who watch me swing.

    The melon I ate for supper
was hard & costly, some merchandiser
knows how to empty his truck
& get out of town fast.
            He's just like you.
He'll be back next summer & fool us again.

Okay, it's the ninth inning & you win again,
you & your natural grass.

                                    But tomorrow's
another day, a whole new game, & I
try to believe my opponent
didnt make the rules.

MOP & SKY

fr Joel Oppenheimer

The house I've fought
is still winning, the new-fangled
gadgets that dont work as well
as their predecessors now in the dump
or some lucky couple's shack,
keep me awake with their metallic
laughter.

                See? You should have stayed with nature,
stupid, she never betrayed
    the heart that loved her, pronoun.

Not true, not true, I say, that love
is simply identification, a loving mind
is a something apart, a step away
from the dewy earth.

But I flush the thousand-dollar toilet
to make it shut up, the pipes running
like a mountain stream in spring.

        If a poem did that, I reply,
I'd dam it, I'd divert it into a pool
for prose cess.
I'd strangle it in its little bed.

But the house is illiterate, cars swoosh by
on the slick avenue, & lift its heart,
not its head from a good book.

FAIR CUCUMBERS

fr Steve McCaffery

The slow eye rarely admires,
the speeding car is a gift
with a brain inside. I am thinking of the sage brush
north of Yakima,
how useless it is to them, how beautiful
if that's a concern.

The cowpoke on the leaping bull
is too busy to count, much less
think, his eye sees nothing, not even
the dollars he might win sometime.

You hear the telephone wires?
Not lately, too busy, your face in a book,
your feet in cow chips for all you know.

The nicest thing about nature
is that it never complains about machines,
if it doesnt like you, too bad, it cant
do anything. Nature is too slow, it doesnt
have a brain, it's like a cat.

"She" is the cat, my auntie always said,
a stickler about pronouns. She was.

No, it may be sage, but it hasnt got a brain;
I havent got a moment
to look back on "the Boy."

MOTEL CONSIDERATION

fr Margaret Atwood

The one more child you never had,
her face appears outside the window,
but when you go outside
only happy birds chitter in their hundreds.
    You need a fierce cat.

Last night I dreamt that I was wakened early
& couldnt get back to sleep,
but when I woke up I knew it
had been a dream I think.

I think of all the fast cars aimed at me,
& a squirrel corpse hanging from a fence.
Time is funny, & difficult
to keep pace with.

                Sitting down, I can travel
nearly as fast as my mind,
but beneath me is the highway
made of a constant formula. It sticks fast
to the surface of the earth, not
to slow me down, me & us,

all you pronouns I dont know, faces
behind the glare of eastward glass.

FACIAL MASSAGE

fr James Schuyler

What is there I have not
forgot? Does that mean seen? Today
I saw Cadillacs & cattle, they did not
herd them. All I heard was the radio,
dumb pick-up truck music. The highway
an interpolation in nature, one
of many.

The sewer-truck man emptied the portable john
& puked good & long onto the road
three days ago in the U.S.A.

Years ago she said you just drive all day,
you never go anyplace. I said the road
is the place. In those days I was twenty-eight
& profound.

                    Now I is this other, I is
a pronoun riding & writing
& mostly writing.

                    The ink used to be nature
or something. It gathers to a smallness
like ancient animals crushed.

I bring it up.

IV

GENTIAN COLOURED FROCK

fr James Schuyler

I stop to inspect the junk
beside the logging truck ranch road,
a piece of some local machine, a red
cigarette package, a Kokanee Beer cap, & finally
a dead calf, its colours perfect,
brown & white, & its legs straight up.

        The Burning University
hundreds of kilometres away, horse mane
clouds, above, I wonder, will someone
eat that calf? Will someone
throw a nosegay of daisies on its grave?

Really it was a highway of sorts,
Number 5, near Aspen Grove, memory
slips into the grave with you, stew
is delicious in September.

        A ruler is a stick
with an unpleasant personality,
just past its end is death, & till then
authority.

        I know a girl kissed a calf
full on the soft lips, little bits of hair
like bp's mustache,
                    a book of cow poems
you wouldnt mind walking in
with bare toes.

DOWN LONG BLACK STEMS

fr Tom Raworth

Dark holds no absence, writing is dark
on what was light, a death
brought to life.

Unjust language
is none of your concern, dont touch
the moving finger in the midst
of its telling.

I hate this heavy thick rain animated
by vengeance, for what? I never did
nothing wrong to you, Cherie, you
just got a bad attitude.

Gentle deer dont complain,
only walk thru the rain & the
light in between, poor illiterate people.

Someone is aiming an overpowered rifle
at you right now, adult Bambi, there
are naked women with your name
& your fortune.

Cities of rain are judgment
on a failed species. What do you think
that pavement was poured over? You'll
never see your granny again.

BROWN CUP, DIRTY GLASSES

fr George Economou

The white wolf hides in the snow,
a line away from blood belonging
to someone else. The flood of mutters
will find him there, betrayed by
a smart-alec scribbler with chilblains.
Whatever they are.

                French novelists
treat life as if it were death, never
carry firearms, talk you to death
at dinner tables.

The white wolf hides under the trees
among the snowflakes, it is early autumn,
the earth tilts & does some people a favour.

        A long female neck, now
talk about snow, a long neck like a penis,
full of blood.

        Why do we let unpleasant images
push in where things were going nicely?

        Why did your favourite family member
choke to death at Christmas dinner?

        Why is death
so damned interesting?

The white wolf hates it
when you write black words all over him.

BUSHY CONSIDERATIONS

fr Anselm Hollo

What smokes a pipe
shoots a deer, didnt hightail it over that deadfall
fast enough, blood on the snow,
black on white in the moon
light.

What smokes a pipe & says
this is not a pipe; we infer
a riddle, bones scattered on a roof.

Up to now it's been easy, too easy for thought,
too loud for the wildlife.

On the Isle of Wight there is no wildlife,
only the strange flesh underground,
the other we all feel reluctant kin to.

Nature
has an inhalation it wants us to exhale,
if we imagine all that rising & falling
as somehow human.

What smokes in a pipe is nature,
& some fool has it in his mouth. He
wants to be a deer, see how fast
he can jump.

I saw him beside the road, feet up
on an apple box. What you selling?

Smoke, he says, smoke & pronouns,
they'll keep you alive.

KITES IN THE WATER

fr Christopher Dewdney

Like Braille on the bark of these blind elms,
all death writing is self-referential.

Writing is death to the fingers,
death all the way up to the shoulders.

Amazement is sometimes a car
that starts at all.

—There's a deer
  hiding behind that tree.
—What kind of tree is it?
—Shit! Now he's gone.

Antlers move thru the bush
like greed in the eye of a Chinese merchant.
He peers across the mist of literature
at our northern forest, his daughter
dances to old Frank Sinatra records.

No one
is dead in this story.

You
might as well have another cigarette,
people used to sing about them on the radio.

Have some nature
rolled up in science.
Make some history.

IT'S ANOTHER MIRACLE

fr bpNichol

All this breathing & blood flow & sometimes
speech, all this becomes a fiction
when you are in a poem. Oh stop
saying "poem" in a poem.

                                                Say "boy."
All right, in a boy. When you are a pronoun
in a watery grave. Everyone is dead.

This is not a story.

I wear a second shirt & call it a jacket.
People remark on the beautiful birds,
they are stitcht on the back. Cats cant get them.
My own back
has been itchy for a week. I dont say this
for the rime (dont say "rime" in a rime),
all right, but it's the immediate fact,
my itching back.

    If I turn around, all this blood flow
& sometime speech will be
ass-frontward, my error when I was five.

I didnt know anything but I was
filled with intelligence. I didnt know
dying but now I'm dying to know.

A ROWBOAT ON FIRE

fr Amiri Baraka

Trembling fate wrapt in flags,
another name for death.
Renewed international respect,
another name for death.
Develop the parklands,
another name for death.

Oh big round eyes, sharp knees in gabardine,
I've seen you all before,
you haunted my teenage years,
your pasty television faces, you know
who I'm talking to?
What a pronoun.

Thought I'd escaped all this, now
I have to grow old, preachers
shouting about Comnewmist music, books
smoking in Ontario, horn-rim senator
axing God to hep him kill four inners.

They're back again, I cant endite poetry
in this kind of world! Listen to this:
a page of ranting.

In the nearly dark sky
silvery clouds remind me
how they said it would be beautiful.

WASH DAY QUESTIONS

fr Gary Snyder

The nightly stroll of raccoons,
dont persuade me re any sub-conscious,
only wide-eyed animal life, like
nothing, only the blood of fiction's
body. There's three of them,
one on the garage roof.

I perish
by night
in holy fire.

No one ever saw
a raccoon waking up,
headlights
fix our hearts on black highways, yellow
stripes are dots if you're fast enough.

Faster still,
they just disappear.

I dont.
I dont want to change pronouns.

When they're dying, everyone
wants to go for one more walk on the ground.

No sense throwing something at those critters.
They'll just take it away with them.

V

BARNACLES & WEDDINGS, ONCE A WEEK

fr James Schuyler

The black & white killer cat who used to live next door walkt my way without seeing or without caring that I was there. He stept four-foot along the rail of the rotting fence, not swaying as it swayed, foot step off the moving board, intent on patrolling my, not his, yard.

A dead mouse I'd meant that morning to throw into the alley was lying flat on its side on the porch. I picked it up by the tail & threw it at the living cat.

He didnt even bother to show he'd noticed, just approacht, jumpt down where the fence turns west, sat on the grass with his ears back, look around.

I was rubbing dead mouse off my finger tip & thumb tip on my jeans. I lifted the finger & pointed it at killer cat & said bang. He fell over sideways with a grin on his face.

Then he rolled over on his back, flipt from side to side like an itchy fish. Did he know the rudiments of etymology and poetic form? No, I holstered my finger. He played for a half a minute.

No one was watching. No one was criticizing. No one ever knew whether we made it all up.

ORDINARY BLUE

fr Gary Snyder

Half a mouse at the door at dawn, so I asked him when he showed up, why do you always start at the head & quit just when you're getting to the fat part? No answer, as usual, just lifts his paw, turns it & starts licking.

I think it's because cats are basically stupid, no matter how they seem to meditate. I picked up the half corpse by the tail & flung it far into the alley, turned my hand & wiped it twenty times on my pyjama bottoms, I'd throw them into the wash.

A human being such as myself, though, up at dawn, cold & moderately happy on the back porch, no one to talk to me, I have always been filled with intelligence, filled with intelligence, like a penis filled with blood.

Like nothing. A squirrel ran along the telephone line over the street, the only squirrel in the neighbourhood. The cat did not know he was there, never lifts his head to look up, afraid something might be looking back.

SILVER DISTURBANCE

fr Robert Creeley

The cat & the squirrel, the one torn, a red thing, & the other somehow immaculate, took me from the world of books to the back alley, never to return. How often I have associated beauty & danger. I had thought of my air force barrack near the end of the runway, lovely night-time explosion of clean beauty into the sky, & then some.

He was the only squirrel in the neighbourhood, you asshole, I said, but like all cats, he wasnt listening to criticism. He hadnt even eaten the head off this time. Mid-day sun glittered on angular refuse in the alley, on the skin too of a fish that may have had tire tracks across it. I lookt up at the telephone wire above the street.

Cats never take a message. They have no experience of amazement. They know nothing of la acción revolucionaria de la mujer. *If we are ever to learn anything from nature, we had better scuff around in the tortured soil of Mars.*

Animals dont die on Mars but they die in "boys" written by gentle westerners. I went into the house & slammed the door. And washt my hands. And admired the curl of water descending slowly from the tap.

FENDERS IN NEW CONDITION

fr Clayton Eshleman

... at the heart of the poem (boy) is no blame. I exited the house, patrolled the back yard, & there were no dead animals anywhere; except the dried corpse of the baby sparrow I left in the unused bird house nailed to the garage wall. Yes, only once in a while do I remember that, less often do I look at it. We are, I remembered, estranged from that with which we are most familiar.

The farther it is from the ground, I reflected, the less quickly nature works its changes. That bird is not a week older in its feathers a year & a half later, it might be sleeping but its head is not under its wing. At the edge of my unusually wide peripheral vision I caught movement; it was either a cat or a symptom of age, or some pronoun. I scanned the back alley, then re-entered the house.

I could feel the house firmly attacht to my back, but I live by day full of faith & courage. One of the firms, I saw by the morning mail, is Vancouver City Savings. I live by afternoons filled with intelligence. Nothing happened that morning, a narrative failure.

SEQUESTERED POP & A STRIPE

fr Stephen Morrissey

Separate from let us say the trees & all that may be living hardly significant lives in them, I stood at the back door, drinking over-cookt coffee & trying to imagine why anyone would dedicate a life to understanding the secret course of nature. I know it gets tedious, you can leave, this rant, & I am no lover of brusht aluminum, well maybe I do have a bit of a crush on it.

A few days earlier I'd seen from the taxi a poor raccoon in a rich neighbourhood, trying to get back across busy Marine Drive. The sun was up & he was late. I dont know whether he made it home but I doubt it. I did. I sat in aluminum & fabric 35,000 feet as they still say in the sky, & I made it home. We burned a billion ancient sea creatures getting here, rings around our eyes in the time differential.

Separate from the earth no more, the blue heron I saw a few minutes later assumed an alternate shape of beauty, a kind of folded sky; who knew what he was looking for? Not eye in the cab, a voice in my head multiplying by one and a half & dividing by ten.

Separate from the boy I am reading & the boy I am writing, I would be nothing but a hairless pronoun cat drinking coffee, I decided, empty of intelligence like a cup stained by old brown acid.

SMALLER & SMALLER, LONGER

fr Judith Fitzgerald

A mere horizontal night was all I had to look forward to when I lockt the back door; two hours later a youth in black would step from nature into invention & take away my video recorder, take away words that used to exist as ideas, now tags to things that shine & are not to be understood but used. What's the use?

It was once easier to abstract, in a Lawrence orchard, a pail of cherries with an agreed weight, a suggested wage, a calculable length of time purchased in the city, next winter. Narrative used to be like that, not like this. Now I pick only a pronoun, a point of view.

From the back porch before I lockt the door I lookt up & saw it from the place my eyes were, a long pale horizon all night. Mere mortals can turn our verses to song, drums not inventing but insisting there's a story can be told over all this beaten grammar. You want out? The door is lockt, you are already out. Build a wall around the self & dont go in.

I had a hard tack in the orchard, just like my dad, il miglior *picker. Now the soft old tree fetches all the light it can in the back yard, cherry pits blancht in the grass around its feet. I go up to lie down, & trees dont, I say out loud, have feet.*

VI

SCOTLAND

fr E.D. Blodgett

To touch your moist
disc of eye

would I
aspire
a rough invention

of mind at last
free from photo
synthesis.

Adjusted language haunts
a mouth dried by
the exit of
speech.

No one ever saw
the last breath
of his cat, no

one ever possessed
one of those that
hairy eared

sequence of triangles
that fear
those muscles touching

one another not
out of mother love
no not at all out.

DISHES

fr Denise Levertov

John the cat
is most my brother

or my self, my
brother forgotten or

far away.
Amazement dims

with distance. Identification
bores me.

She's the cat,
I'm the me. Never

look too long at John
or he'll be gone.

Why I'm drawn over
& over to the porch

I dont know. I
turn my face & there's

the moon, weak
as I've seen her.

She's a pronoun
in the night sky, an

insistent trope im-
patient of tropism.

Me too,
& John.

WHEY

fr Tom Clark

The burning
university

is the figure,
distant

handsome guys
are the ground.

Who are they,
why are they

doing that?
Let's look

elsewhere, I see
with my moist eye

something that is
dead. Guess

the meaning of life
yourself, deadeye,

look hard
into the flames, those

handsome guys are
cool cats, Jewish

in deportment,
triangular, safe.

SIDE

fr Michael McClure

Black sheep move
thru the deep
snow

        no
matter how
we call them

truly stupid
nature, beautiful
in the moon

light as a moth
on paper. You

write? So do I
my friend, quiet

as a mouse
in the gaze

of a cat. Black
sheep move without

sound, too far away
for the grind of

teeth, smooth
in your eye.

The snow will
never melt, never
pounce the cat.

MOLLUSC

fr Tom Raworth

Heart
and heart
so far
a
part

so fast
the car
that glides
a way.

Nature, dear
Mom
never be-
trayed

the heart
that loved
her

was her.
A part

of what,
of an I

dentification?

THOUGHT, INC.

fr David Cull

Flurry of
apple blossoms

white on black, what
is the
black?

Is someone
clearing her throat?

No questions
now in this
short boy,

let us instead
admit
defeat. But

that image, ah
it wasnt
mine.

When
is it
ever?

Never, but
is that
consoling?

There, you
did it
again,
pronoun.

SHEETS

fr Jon Furberg

All mortal
kindness
sunk

in hollow
skull,

gold of flesh
skinned away,
essential

property leans
on death
knowledge.

A large
shadow
falls over me

& before me
lies wisdom

wont
last long
enough

of this I
am sure
& I
also,

& kind.

VII

THE RIGHT HORSE

fr Bryher

If certain seekers still
call reason sweet, what was our real
destiny but hazard?

You step for no reason
back onto the curb and she just
misses you in her long low car.

I didnt see, I was looking
the other way, didnt hear, didnt know
what night it was.

Buy me what you want to buy me,
show me your swordplay, call me
any person you desire,

I'll be there, I and I, tooth
gleaming with a recent drink,
I'll be there, too, I'll be you.

When we are both lying dead,
having lost at length, I'll be there,
I'll be you.

FORTY-NINE FLAGS

fr Louis Zukofsky

He wished that the raindrops on the flower
would reflect as tears in his eyes,

wished now and again for ever it seemed
but only a moment was, the chair

overturned, the occupant of a moment
gone. He wished it were a film

they starred in or a film over his eyes,
reflecting tears in a flower's cup.

No such luck, the lips like petals
crushed were gone or never were.

He opened his and spoke in the cool
night after rain, he heard someone say

she'll be there, she and she, tooth
gleaming with a recent downpour,
she'll be there, too, she'll be you.

When you are both lying dead,
having lost at length, she'll be there,
she'll be you.

THE LANDING

fr Gertrude Stein

In every country in some way it is
not right to be dead, that is to die.

I go away,
I shop at the IGA,

I go a gain,
I grow any way.

In every country in some way
the flowers survive our hatred,

we go to the grocery store
and observe vegetables cut from their stems.

We peer closely at a carrot
in a cello bag, it's been passed by, but

it'll be there, it and it too,
gleaming from a recent clerk misting,
it'll be there, true, it'll be you.

When you are both lying dead,
having lost at life, it'll be there,
it'll be you.

THAI ROPE

fr H.D.

I want you to match the flowers
along your terraces. Want you

to remember what smokes a pipe
and stay away from it. What grows

is for life and beauty, whoever thought
I'd be invoking their names? Are they

names? Can you give names to what
are not things? The flowers along your

gown's edge, they distract me
from my hatred, attract me

to nature's yearning for human company.
Make me nearly desire to be human, say

I'll be there, you and I, truth
gleaming with a decent reserve,
I'll be there, to love and comfort you.

When we are both dying, dying,
having lost at love, I'll be there,
I'll be smoke.

FENDER PAINT

fr Hubert Aquin

Crouched dully over paper as white
as the sheet with which one hangs
oneself, I know I'll never be my grand-dad.

Never be a blue note coming from
the other's hilly south. I'll never
see Mo'orea again, dont have any

relatives in Switzerland anymore. I
crouch over this gift paper, black now
on white, like a zebra in the snow.

Like a doomed intercontinental agent,
dont know anything about death
poetry, just go night by night, holy.

I'll be here, I and I, night
glowing with a stupid dread,
I'll be here, too, I'll be it.

In this vapid game of tag,
having won at last, I'll be grand,
I'll be dead.

RECKONING RIGHT

fr Samuel Beckett

The lids occult the longed-for eyes,
hidden world, where is it, meaning
who has them, meaning lost yet

or meaning escaped, all fires the fire
I read in a dream, a child dreaming
eyes open in my dream, closed to

my father's possible midnight gaze.
I wonder whether he ever, actually,
did. When he wasnt looking a cat

nobody knew well lay on my mouth
and suffocated me in my sleep. She
was not even supposed to be there.

She was there, she and she, youth
warming through her quiet body,
she was there, too, she's the cat.

When we were both lying dead
and dreaming, only she was there,
she was not longed-for.

SOFT GUMS

fr Charles Reznikoff

Without the glitter of an apt word or thought
he walked back up to the flat, a squashed man
at the end of his game. Words followed

a few paces behind, like cats interested
but uninclined to show it. Leaning
on his hungry look, he opened the door,

checked the bits of nature secured in pots,
checked the locks on the windows, rejected
suicide, idly bent to brush an animal.

It is not gold, he thought, not all of it,
none of it as precious as a long neck, long
legs scissored for a moment, stepping from the car.

We'll be there, we and we, royal,
shining like an editor born,
we'll be there, too, we'll be you.

Like you, we are fit to be praised,
having left at length, we'll be you,
you'll be there.

CIRCULAR FENCES

fr Herman Melville

One neither courting nor shunning regard,
but evenly pursuing the path of duty,

I will await delayed mercenaries, off-
centre target on my chest, braving nothing

so much as the weather, an air
filled with razors nobody shaves with.

I wait like a committee for decisions
that will not concern me, at night

I lie back in holy fire, not my recompense
but the bed we were all born on.

I seize my personal pronoun and dream,
dreaming a sleeping verse, your instructions.

You'll be there, you and you, high
on the top side of an unnoticed rime
you'll be there, why, you'll be home.

When you are all newly born,
in the light of another wakeful planet,
you'll be born.

Everything else will be nature.

Do Sink

Calgary and Vancouver
July–August 1991

(Pomflit, 1992)

1

When I have fears that I
may cease to be
open to pain that shines
wet on the side of a gold
fish in my own, I thought,
pond

        I ought to forget
comfort, forget family
history, drive a black sedan
over thin prairie roads
looking for a town even
my mother does not believe
was ever there

                    knowing
pain is not colour, not value
but condition, the cost
of starting a damned life in
the first place, where no
thinking man ever was.

2

Before my pen has
gleaned my teeming brain
the vehicle of forget all this
piece by piece will pull up
from behind, an unremembered
cousin at the wheel

                                        coloured
like the car and beautiful
in a tailored shirt, forget
that and that and that thing
you've not quite recalled,
take my hand

                                & souls of poets
long since gone sit down to sing
with your family, did you think
you could just grow those
upper arms, wait for a bus, and get
whisked away beyond pain?

3

Before high-piled books,
in charactery this fool
scribes his day, walks the town
as if new to the job without
rising from his desk, a black car
parked in back

                    with orange cats
coiled on the warm hood, his team
of familiars, his destiny, nine
lifetimes prepared hopelessly, this
idiot with a black pen writes
and yet writes

                    with ginger
in his shadowed heart, protected
from the sun and its rays, the
measure of the year a few lines
that will last longer than a cherry
tree bird's song.

4

Driving a dusty black sedan
over flimsy prairie roads,
he feels his eyes and mind's machine
hold like rich gamers
the full ripened grain, the
dark void of night

                                        somewhere
high behind him, while family
never met will rush from ground
like wheat into a lovely maiden's
hand, her picture now the reverse
of our currency

                                  dropped from our
fingers faster and faster as we age,
dirt from our skin piled into heaps
to rival these small prairie hills, loam
to grow a grandmother, obfuscate
a self.

5

When I behold, upon the night's
starred face, a gold sheen, I know
my eyes are old beyond their desire,
two aged deer as dull as the surface
of this pond

I contemplate
falling into, when I behold
no star's reflection on that face
I hate the books piled high
that told me heaven was
what we worked for, fame
was love

deferred, a family
wider than a suburb firmament,
a story we must aid the telling of,
we must edit with our
failing breath.

6

Huge cloudy symbols of a high
romance in the night sky shimmer,
images of satisfied self-murder
haunt one's eyes inside the windshield
on the prairie, drive he said, everyone
insane

            with melodious chuckle
in strings heard from rear speakers,
laughter beside a dark road dangerous
& narrow under starlight, families
emerging from hard soil, weed roots
sliding from their shoulders

                                        weak
from disuse, exactly what the thrush,
could he have spoken, would have said,
an observant eye in available light, a
relative bird awake when one is nearly
asleep at the wheel.

7

I'm driving this black sedan
too swiftly over rutted prairie roads
and think that I may never live to trace
my DNA another generation
down the route of fate, oh damn
such maunderings

                                        come upon so early
in the dying business, before my pen
has gleaned a thing worth harvesting,
or so one says every year, and considers
a grandmother who likely never wrote at all
save misspelled letters to her sister

lost to the south, caught in a draught
no one could have expected, deep
in another family, wild shoeless brothers
with big noses, my kin, my *semblables,*
too dear to keep in memory, in a line
that grows longer as we walk it.

8

Driving under dark prairie clouds
I confuse their shadows with
the magic hand of chance, lose
all trace of grandparents to the geography,
the ground converted

in the vehicular
mind into latitudes, for instance,
of mortality, no matter the voices
alongside the road, no matter the urgings
of the season, haunting is haunting, dying
is less exciting as it goes

along, looking
for whatever it looks for, chromosomes,
colours of late seasons, cruel anemones, perhaps
spouting out of literature with comic face,
comic mice under those nearby leaves,
I think they are, racing by.

9

And when I feel, fair
creature of an hour, brought up
so rudely from the earth, that I
will never see you plain, your whispering
by the roadside like the night breeze
in thistles

seems to propel this black
vehicle, no star's reflection on its back,
an almost unseen shark in the gloom,
and in its belly a tiring brain that wants only
some abandoned town you lived in
too young to know its name

and then dead
too soon to hear of mine, oh a sentence
can never be as confused as our line, the
unknowing all along it, the progeny
suffering in silence some pain for one actual,
for the next a story being told.

10

I'm scared to death that I shall never
look upon thee more clear than
I do tonight, dark creature of a time
long past my memory, long past the desire
of my mother's recollection, who never
heard these roadside ditches sing

this song
like thistles, like music scribed by pens
gleaning brains we would never recognize
even were their headstones to be found
in that pine-bordered plot in the middle
of the bald-headed

where a black sedan
parked in westering sunlight while this
lorn grandson walked hopeless and lost
on his DNA's purported earth again, you
nowhere to be found inside that square, only
encountered in the roadside's bright dirge.

11

Locked inside this heavy car, I will
never have relish in the faery
power known to the unknown who
walked this way in a musical past, never
ride the vehicle invisible beyond desire,
never remember

where my share of
molecules might fetch up, D for desire,
N for Never, and A for a beginning we
all have honestly missed, watching
intently as we can the roadside slippage,
the willows in the wind

that is only
main component of our song, oh what ears
we waste on one another's plaints, oh
what hours we cast aside while our dearest
family dies in other arms, oh how late
we come to realize or not.

12

When I perceive the prairie beside the road
as a pond of unreflecting love—
then on the shore far from this dark
the night sky falls to wrap those quick
golden shapes

                                        that swim like thought
where we seek no mother's mother, here
beneath the still wheels of this dark sedan
are bones enough, unbending below
their burden of invisible earth, stones
caught in the arms of soil

                                                                        some tried
to instruct us has always been the base
of our being, while we, riders
of pneumatic spin, cast our loyalty
to an idea, God is Love, Mother
is Queen of Earth, Dian of Heaven
and whatever that is out there.

13

I remember this night, getting out
of the car to wait: in the reputed centre
of the wide world I stand alone, and think
like a sheen of gold-sided fish, flitting
into the dark, no stars in this crown, no
supreme darkness

to see them in, a voice
by the side of the road is only the weather,
no stone marks a grave if it is here,
the dying business is not tidy, ruts in the road
are direction, not aid, the end of light
is partly darkness only

given to grandsons
who cannot turn their eyes to look inward,
and will forget the time they tried, have fears
that themselves will cease to be, when suns
rise and bring partial light, gold at first, a
flash of lesser metal, a day.

14

When I have fear that eyes may
cease to be upon me, looking only through
what seems to be there, here, in the centre
of the shadowed earth nearly flat with age,
oh then what seems to me a mother's mother
is only the mother

                    of these late thoughts,
what vehicle brings us to this halt, what spectre
carriage with what geography implied, oh
let me remain outside, above the maternal ground
of being, below the dark clouds of seeming,
inside any out there is

                        relative to what
there is not, let me start the engine and release
anything, the clutch, the earthlike hold of bones,
release the music of the roadside ditches, back
let me go, let me rouse my fancied kin and think
till song and pain to nothingness do sink.

Blonds on Bikes

Aarhus, etc.
October–December 1995

(Talonbooks, 1997)

1

Blonde on a bike—

mer mer murderous,
silent in October dark

—whoops of my heart.
I'm too old for
these long night walks—

dog bark
ring bell
streets, building

how old in North Sea
oughta be quiet,
no

that noiseless
wheel and wheel
didnt touch a leaf
a dry eye

my stride

2

Mist every morn, we're
north, narrow streets
and stone

—blonds on bikes, oh for a
drop of the south—

                                        pah! this
is someone's south, my
east,
          no sea between
anything.

                              Mind scurries
like a bike in the north
downhill,

                              time all over
my arms, hair tangled
in the hours,
                              my my my
possessions

                              scattered
across the globe,
                                        the
hilly streets

3

Long loping dark *gades*
no bus rides

no city glow in sky,
long heart trips over
arrow ocean arcs in
gone night, where
seagulls? where
rest of body? where
brain doesnt want cigarettes

—long dark streets all
downhill from everywhere
another heart hid
behind Nordic stones,

windows with books behind ’em

4

—short hair, short hair
short hair & wire eye glasses

eye glasses all round
they're on bikes, wear
boots,
          look like them
selves,

          she said oh all
those beautiful blondes,
                              who cares
about—

            Oh there goes one
now, sits feet on chair
looks at his bandage,

                              ah,
imperfect!

5

Late breakfast beer
young students primp, instructional
youth glug gesture,
smoke
between fingers, I dont see
myself here
at all

not at all, tall skinny
kid, years later she said
was beautiful—
how come
no one
ever tol' me, would I
believe myself—

some old coot
watching me drink beer
in mystic pub
downtown
Friday night
twenty-five cents
in my pocket

6

Never find yr way
  round Aarhus,

  standing in forlorn bus shelter
  outside a town, wrong
  way Bowering, shoulders ache
  carrying groceries

 hard rain whips in waves
 down important highway,

    goof looks for number 17 bus
    going right way, it's

    a peninsula 'tween storms

    —who can read oh mercy
    a number thru wet specs,

    who said this lorn wet man
    had the brains to get

    invited?

7

Lunch by a cold lake,
no, it’s an ocean, flat,

boat with fishermen,

                                        lunch is
schnapps, what a good Sunday,

what a son, welcome back
numero uno,
                        master,
two of them,

                            sausage &
savage &
red cabbage, heavy rye bread,

beer from squat dark bottle,
woman looks over her specs

—what could be more sabbath,
less work—?

8

Bright bright bright, my boy
the sun,

window's open
Nordic sea air creeps in—

October, not scary up here
beside Scotland,
no low
ghost of dark ice,

it's bikes
on the tarmac,
it's cool, Mac,

we write till our veins are empty

words bright as wind,
powerful as blocks of wood,

lonely as a candy
in the gutter

9

Salty licorice, remember?

goes with hunch
over notebook

walks across the park
where ducks make voices loud
as any Dane—

licorice, they
love it, it comes all shapes
all salty,

their sea demands
no less,
their blood
salty as a breakfast
rollmop,

they make a hundred
sweet buns,
but salt is their
bottom
nature

10

Lone longhair, dark jeans,
blunt boots,
hunch over coffee—

they leave him alone, these
blond boys
with naked ears

—war's over fifty years, Jutland
rocks now
to *guitarros* held
like cellphones,

where's the famous
pornography,
forget it, forget

British battleships
welcome
in, this is no-time,
the end
of your century,
ol' bub

11

Goof goes out under sun,
gets rained on

goes on right bus
gets lost near weeds—

Orders food he cant read,
finds it delicious

lives just to the side
of his head

under grey sky with
an edge somewhere

dreams of wide ocean
pocked with raindrops

streaks on plane window—
behind his glasses, too

12

Looking for a red & white bike
    girl with strong arms
    skinny & pocked
                                hardly at all—

she's nobody in the world
        a fixture here in heaven

no one to him, a corporeal
wraith, a memory,   a
        kid's far friend—

but black bikes quiet as air
    nearly kill him on Nørrebrogade
    downhill to post office

    a step sideways is death,
      face in concrete
          among his own
                sunflower seeds—

how trivial life is,
   how fine

13

It's rock at last, sea water,
    actual *wood*iness
                              back again
Norge or home, or is this my name?

Brinson
          —Granddad's big bulby nose,

Mom's deep set eyes, hillbilly
        far from home
                  or right there

a pine tree behind us, gulf-
stream in our
                  Arkansas blood?

—no time for questions, here
      gotta walk, no rain
      no snow,
                    Bergen fjord,
call it bear won,
                      say no goldilocks
got a chance
        when I got my sweater on

14

Sittin' in Bergen
watch sumo on TV
from France—

I been on this rock
a long time,

quick moves, easy passage,

slicked back hair,
gotta eat some lettuce,

lead with my head—

he writes to himself
literally,

sheen of hair
on tube,
squeeze out
years on this cold ocean,

spit sunflower seeds
on Olav Kyres Gate

15

Klee eighty—

a lone hand's held up,
fingers curled a bit,
the thumb cut off

—moon is near,
I want it   I want it

I only seem to have it
where it's dark,

a black house is empty,
the paint cracks gently,

the white cross
stands in darkness?
What
order
here
& there—

this is a story
of the
and a

16

Here's Tonje Larsen
another caprice
                    on hardwood

sweet heavy height
& turbine leg powers,   up

& sling, the ball's
   in the net,

                  that sweaty
smile, the Swedes dont do that—

these wonderful Norge girls,
big flesh,
            Tonje looks like

Owen Curnoe, no sylph she

bashes her sweet way
      into your heart

               learning the rules

17

—become for the weekend
a carnivore,
poor sauced-up
caribou here yclept
reindeer
red all through
her meat
slithers in me—

we three
walk in fjord rain,
climb fence,
marvel at our three languages

—the north of sixty oldsters?

no, meat eaters, wild
as Norse,
hardy as handball
queens

18

Atlantic somewhere,
        somewhere past there

up in ceiling, how far
        are those rain clouds

how far from home, oh
        blonds on bicycles

        tell me how young
        this country is

                used to
conquer whatever were left over,
        a bitty island here,

          some ice there, a

   green spot from time to time

            a German *Fußball* team

19

Bright blue sky
not needed,
it's in their eye—

I'm a dark thing
from the west
a grey

ocean swept up & left
like breakfast fish
nobody eats

a simile from the east of the east

the least likely food
for bicycle kids—

but they look,
those eyes dont turn away,

they are new children
from the just this minute
risen soil

20

Woman next door
        used to be surly,

    now she's a Finn
    lost in language
                        as I am,

puttin' cheese on her bread

leavin' keys on the table

never said please in her life—

she's
the rain, light but ready

as we're learning to be
here in the Nord
                after all—

me too, gottadmit it,
lost over America

found wanting
        in Jutland

21

A graph of the mind
fidgetting,

bones
articulate thought & I wake up
unable to walk—

How about
growing old,
that's an
option?

Well, I
used to think so

—too old to be a hunter
I gotta learn to be
a story teller,

when over here
I remember stuff
you'll never care about—

I used to drive a green Chevy
Bel Air

22

Wears glasses when he writes now,
plays softball with blood on his face,

thinks of home, the shower, the kitchen
when he's in Europa's
        stony embrace—

But I love it,
I love streets with cobbles
used to have blood between 'em,
clang of dropt sword

—November sun weak
        in old Nord Europe

muffled people lean on their wind,
beer gets dark in corners,
        step down to
                electric heaters

—old babies got no hair,
no sense of home

23

Sky in Europe's
        full of airplanes,

aero-planes

traffic as on the street
taking little bits
                of human room

& travellers hurry to get up there,
fill the sky with Danes & Greeks

get the population half in the air

fossil fuel cascading to earth
film over blonds on bikes

living with snakes & publishers
on the ground,
                lining up

to get into sky metal

24

Dont exactly yodel
        but they talk loud,
laugh like their guts are coming out

slam chairs around
thump into people or nearly

these Nords, agh, they
            look okay
        they vote okay

            but stay outa their elevator
            & bicycle path,

listen to the wind
        early at night
            brings the Atlantic
cleans the toes or town

  bends your knees
    & makes you say please
  makes you lean

  quietly into November

25

Stony face woman
          beautiful as a knife

says yr outa that room—

I'm an old helpless fart
     say what'll I do

     bad enough I have to
     get up at four—

She might have fucked a prince
          one year, says
               I have a new tenant—

I slump my shoulders,
          cant get it up for a princess

I'll eat breakfast in a hotel
          but no herring
               I dont care
                    what colour

26

They laugh loud,
they have a secret method
for talking loud

loud

the ducks are loud
in their nightglow pond

little kids
cry loud on Frederiksgade—

I jump when the moron
opens his huge mouth
and loud food comes out

I'm in a hurry
but they're loud

the trucks roar on Nørrebrogade

but a silent bicycle
can kill you quick

27

Sittin' under my hat
in Frankfurt Hauptbahnhof

wondering how in *Himmel*
Kroetsch got lost—

it's another fiction,
guy'll do anything
for a trope

lose himself in a shower,
lose himself
while Paul Bley
looks for the next
note

—hide from them women
in nice coats
asking for money
for their babies

28

No law against it
in the European community

stay in bed all day
dont flush the toilet

use all the hot water

—you're a long way from home
or dead,
a long way from dead

—it's cold, I mean,
out there
a silver glint
on that roof,

what did
your mother say?
dont go
asking for trouble

oh yes, and
stay out of the river

29

Sittin' on the DSB
beside four Turks
playin' hearts—

the guy across from me smiles
& the guy beside me
blows his chance
to take control

uses his king of spades
before the queen's out
& swallows thirteen points

—German orchard zooms
by the windows

& in the Okanagan
long November nights
the folks with Kraut names

wile away the time
over pasteboards

—I can taste
bratwurst
on my teeth

30

I'm looking at German trees
    through the eyeglasses

    of the Japanese guy
            looking out the window,

now I realize
    I'm wearing glasses too

                    or who
                        am I
                            trying to fool

writing in a ruled
            Italian notebook

        a Canadian gave
            me in Toronto
                twenty years ago—

uh huh
    those trees:

        if you cant whup um
        keek um
        & if you cant keek um
        gum them mothers to death

31

Lookin' at people
on the Frankfurt S-Bahn

it's hard to figure how
Hitler dreamed of a master race

—the one blond guy with Aryan face
has an earring
on the gay side

32

Here 'n the north
bright sun off
icy old snow

it's something like home
you slept thru

dozed all yr years
dreaming you were
somewhere else

in the rain—

Blonde comes to the door
and talks herself into a poem

in like manner

—born god knows where
in a dream
where there is no phone line

to the outside world

33

Candy all over the desk,
that's a traveller's diet

dreams of home you've never seen
blue sky hanging off the Ritz

a clock insisting on this
strange time—

birds cant find you,
neither can your mum,

it's like that thing you
were afraid of
coming
after childhood

34

Heidelberg,
it says Canada
on every wall
every fence

couldnt get away
from Canada

a sweet
broken old *Schloss* on the hill
lit me up for a while

I got away from home

I never saw Bing Crosby
in a stupid hat
he makes look good

—I had a little beer
for its name

never tried
to get away
from that

35

Gets all
    gets law
        gets lost

in yellow buses
        out in zone 3

the country, Jylland
         dark
on its snow

      sitting like a guy
in his green raincoat

alone on the number 9
   for instance
         past the city
limit
   into law

all
  lost
    on a peninsula

going to get gobbled
    by Norway

          the law
of the frozen jungle

36

Hello, son

long shadows
cut ducks in half

arouse shouts of winter glee
like hee hee
from gaggles of free school kids,

sun just above the trees
hanging on to four leaves each,

everything measured carefully

in Nord land

my eyeblinks, twenty an hour

insects counting each other
in their warm woodpiles—

I have beaten my dreams

I'm lending form to them

they dont even know

what I mean

37

American news
it makes an ooze

as far as I can see
all over the world

suggesting
expensive hotels,
gonna tell you

how important Bosnia has become
from a U.S. eye

and is there
another?

—makes you talk silly
makes you write
crippled ridicule

makes you
go for a Danish breakfast

fast

38

White beard elves
in Copenhagen airport
twitch back & forth

to muzak *Jule* songs,

no wonder all the men
are guzzling beer

no wonder I'm reading WCW
in German,
no wonder

left on the Nord world
at all,

let me
I say
outta here,

I cant afford
forty kroner
for a beer

39

Keep seeing David W. McFadden
in Europe's airports,

today I saw a Chinese one
in Frankfurt, how

does he do it?

comes toward me
like a tuatara

a trick
he picked up

in a New Zealand airport.

bad enough I see
his friendly lizard face
on Bloor Street,

what's he doing over here?
and why does he
smile a little
& pass on by?

40

The only known human
who's had only
terrible meals in Bologna,

kinda thing never
makes it into
his writing,

ol' Spartan
dont care,
got free
toothpick
on airplane

thinking of burger day
back home

grease on fries
here & there

flies on grease
oozing like American news
from his grave

41

Cross this water
    Bosnians kneel in snow,

    go,   go
            south, get
                west of here

    go north
          get out
              of a plane—

    I's your face, Paddy,
          you look white & pink here,

    —Italian women
          show their legs
              & they dont have
                    great legs

    but to show them,
          no wonder I have
                W.C. Williams in a bag,

    he'd know why
          & he'd love 'em

42

The good folk of Rimini
just use the Roman bridge
to get across town

pass under the Roman arch
to go shopping—

dov'è l'Italia?
come posso trovarla nella mia mente
se la mia mente non ha fine?

—well, on the train
you learn to stand up
before your stop,

them Romans taught us all
to be there on time

43

On the climb
in genial
San Marino

one sees in shop window
a Buffalo Bills Zippo,

old folks climb
with canes
and good clothes

rock getting higher & higher
as little guys
put up

cement high rise building
preposterous
redundancy

in square sky

44

Saw my sister
          on Pescara train

didnt speak to her
          watching Sally's face

looking at her familiar gestures
          and face expressions

those eyes I've known
          fifty summat years

looking right at me
          along real
                blur Adriatica

45

Take it back, the
sun warms us here
& in Pescara

young women's legs
are terrific—

everyone's old wears black,
everyone's young & sexy wears black,

in between it's another world
full of parliamentarians
& lady professors in
sharp eye glasses

—I meanwhile
keep an eye open
for a warm place to shit

and enemy aircraft

46

Bright birthday sun

it's warm as summer
in Roma

cats
hide under cars,
dogs
are on leashes
held by self-conscious

women

—one stood next to me
loveable and rank,

a time for
literary consideration,

now I spose
I'm old

forgot my comb
came as I am

as if I'd earned it

47

Italian intellectuals
    are the nicest audience,

you feel like a poet
    reading to them

    reading, a voice in Rome
        from strange space—

The rooms are
    inside a door
        off a bent brown *vincola*

you'd never find
    with your favourite dog

—you wear black clothes
    because they're yours

    you read words
        your youth knew

48

They're kissin' at the station,
        ones that dont
                have to carry my bags,

I carry,
          used to kiss

used to not be in Rome

used to write
    between kisses

    now get a fax

    & cant read it,
           now study

spits of rain
        on the eyeglasses

front of me

49

Blankets of little birds
rise from fields

as Bologna
train goes by,

there's always
one little black sheep

alone,

white wool circle,
black pupil

50

Bright like they say
necklace

natale lights
in Bologna
night streets,

what's that weird music?

shepherd pipes
in designer
via d'Azeglio—

how can they wear those costumes

so un-
selfconscious, a 1995

cook pot
you never been in

so far from New Brunswick,
from Sharon Stone
her crudity

51

Sittin' alone in restaurants
        all over the continent,

here I nibble my breadstick
        etc.
                and watch this lone fat woman

has a big beer
eats a whole pizza
forks her way through
        a big gloppy cake

examines the conto
        with a scowl

—but ol' continent man
        I didnt think the ravioli
              would be so many,
        had no idea
              the *scallope* with artichokes sauce
        would be so big,

              could hardly get through the door
              from Italy,

        looked down, the Austrian Alps
              covered with white

              didnt feel hungry at all

53

Every second corner
St. Nick's
handin' out *Erdnüssen* & oranges

outa big burlap sacks,

kids dont say a word

they are earth
with eyes

just old enough
for Nick's day

in old Nazi cities

ancient good cheer,
big expectations,

Nick's ponies
stand front of cart,

they used to be little,
still are,
still are ground

in the city

54

Just cold enough
for an old lady
bent back

on two canes
in dark street Frankfurt

headed for stony church
or smoky corner bar,

got some old underwear
I hope

a secret
from all Americas

55

Eats Italian
in big German city
every night

Jawohl
mein Herr
and another *Bier*

cant even shake
Europe's dust
in this froze

oh so froze
he cant reach in pockets
for gloves—

these Chermans, though,
warm, filled with
swine *Fleisch*,

oh Christmas
sausages, oh
D.H. Lawrence

swing of emotion,
oh hate & love
this Europe where few
wars are

56

Lots of weird people
near the door
of lorn Frankfurt station

but how could you
get lost here?

I'm wearing my own hat,
carrying too many bags
for personal defence

give myself up to
air
& the knives

in the air—

comin' home
with sore heart,
aching shoulders

frantic arithmetic
for my fellow Canucks

His Life

Vancouver
1988–1998

(ECW, 2000)

SUMMER 1958. MERRITT

Days below the forest are becoming
hot, hot, hot, tritely
hot. Childhood days, when eating too much
is horrific.

Exploded words, like trees in a fire
cresting. Similies scarring a book,
not a sail in sight.

A letter from J. He wonders whether she
thinks of him. She didnt even sculpt him.
She can do whatever she wants to him.
He wonders if he'll see her again.

His grades have been mailed. He's doubly
anxious to see them. His, too. He wonders if
his father outdid him again.
                    Classical
relation makes a family of us all.

FALL 1958. VANCOUVER

First day of lectures
in his third year of study

and Malcolm was alive,
Lowry, city full of parks.

It could have been his sixth year
but he regrets nothing, life

goes like episodes, Yankees win
again, dogs bark from wet yards.

They live on 20th near Oak Street,
where Jews go to the meat store,

the best writer in town is still
alive, mountains and their scant trees

far away. No one
is swinging a bat, the wet fields

have soccer posts, painted white
every year. The old loves, habitual

friendships, old memories re-enclose,
re-awake. But those books, ah

God.

WINTER 1958. OLIVER

A legend
beginning to fade,
a noisy family
in a town without snow.

He cant flick his ashes in the fireplace.
It is a new electric heater.
You have entered the hill-straits—
a sea treads upon the hill-slopes.
There is nothing exactly
to do all day.
And yesterday went with the ice.

SPRING 1959. VANCOUVER

The National Hockey League with its
normality ends its season tomorrow, maybe
the Leafs will finish
fourth.

He's reading T.S. Eliot, as usual
enjoying the images, jumping off
the train.

He recorded his five-pin
bowling scores, with J the left-handed,
166–119, 116–145, 232–107. Life
is sweet.

The city any time
can expect sunshine and warmth. This
is life, nor is he eager
for now
to get out of it.

Banality is all right, competition
is something like poetry, it lasts
for a second, and it means
nothing but itself.

SUMMER 1959. OLIVER

They drove up to a mosquito-infested spot
this side of Bridesville for a picnic,
for the wind on the hills,
the low hill is spattered
with loose earth—

Chico rolled in wet cow manure
so he threw him into a creek twice.
He was sorry.

Below, there is, they see,
a beauty in this valley,
where the earth is largely stone.

FALL 1959. VANCOUVER

The history prof is much the same this year.
The political science prof is quite dull

as a hyacinth,
hidden in a far valley,
perishes upon burnt grass.

The leaves are still on the trees, most
of them green in the wind

that turns them, to look them over.
The English prof is a ludicrously pompous

poseur.

                    We all perish
before the streets are too wet for sparks.

WINTER 1959. OLIVER

He and Willy had a few beers
at the Oliver hotel. Then they drove
Windy Bone & the other Indian to their horses.

What note shall we pitch?
We have a song,
on the bank we share our arrows;
the loosed string tells our note.

Sally is working nights and he is working days.
They havent seen one another for a long time.
Apparently a man died in her arms last night.

No coffee or poetry for him any more.
No more buzzing words in his ear.

Willy wondered whether they would see them
leave. But Windy
wanted them to ride their horses in the crisp moon.

No, they said, thank you, Windy, but no.

SPRING 1960. VANCOUVER

He bought a baseball glove
and a book of poems,

he saw Warren Tallman with his
omnipresent coffee thermos.

How many times a day do you fill that up, he asked.
Enough to keep me percolatin', was the reply.

You cannot win the Nobel Prize
playing baseball. Cannot call the muse.

O flight,
bring her swiftly to our song.

Desolación
by Gabriela Mistral.

The coffee keeps us awake.
The poems wake us up.

SUMMER 1960. VANCOUVER

A widening circle of world
takes him downtown for a second time today,

to the art gallery, there's Tessai
on paper, there's an old bishop

lecturing in Japanese, tough samurai voice
and tiny yellow head, nearly transparent,

bends this ancient pottery head over paper,
his purple robe falling exact.

Young B's knuckles feel like rough bolts,
his pants feel sticky in the middle.

Bishop was Tessai's chief student, students
come in all sizes. Now he's doing calligraphics

and young B'll get one, it'll be there
on his study wall when he's someone else

remembering a silver watch on the old man's thin left wrist,
the Nisei girl flattening rice paper for his quick brush,

remembering he nearly expired
each time he saw her angelic breasts.

FALL 1960. VANCOUVER

First month of lectures
in his fifth year of studies

in early morning sleep time
high on the second storey

of someone else's house,
for the first time since he wore a hat

he pissed the bed. Had to
bundle sheets to the laundromat.

She said he has been running fast
to the toilet lately, he might have

a bladder infection. He might years later
write a poem containing

history or a bladder infection. They ride to school
on bicycles, which is fine

but damned wet on head and legs
in the Autumn West Point Grey rain.

WINTER 1960. OLIVER

Night after night of liquor,
oily stuff in his clothes.

Waiting for the Greyhound bus,
they went bowling. She bowled

while he went for a mickey of rum,
then they bowled, poor things.

Five pins.

> *The hard sand breaks,*
> *and the grains of it*
> *are clear as wine.*

She dropt his bottle splash on the floor.
It was partly for the bus.

He went for another
while she bowled some more.

He always writes down his scores,
but not in poems. She had a pull

on the bottle, a push on him.

SPRING 1961. VANCOUVER

Exploration an easy trope,
the new so tiring, the sweet
so near;
                that is he partied with her
for twenty-four hours, it was
Corinna's twenty-first birthday, her swain
forty-five, English, an actor, let our hero
drive his Daimler, rev its
Rolls-Royce motor.
                                    They drank at her place
till eleven, caught Rolf Harris
at the Arctic Club, heard the Mary Kaye Trio
at the Cave, dined and danced
at the Penthouse, champagne
till breakfast, champagne
for breakfast.
                            Life with her
was always like this, champagne and peaches
for lunch, music and games
all day,
                till they had to rush,
to make a dinner date,
sip drinks surrounded by polished wood.

If he was going to be what he was,
he could continue this Rolls-Royce life
or something else,
                                would he continue
something else?

SUMMER 1961. OLIVER

The sun is down, he stands
fully awake
                                        and wonders what sleep is

in this vapidity, no one
living in his home town desires

anything but the new television,
they wish to see no further

than a man on a horse, a man
with a gun, a father who after all

did know best.
                                              He, on the other hand,
knows nothing, he's twenty-five, he

was the only person in the house
who watched *The Human Voice* of

Cocteau last night. He's writing a novel,
he thinks, no one else does, but

he only watches the ball game, he
keeps score and announces the hitters.

He likes the word "cerebral," he
uses it while characterizing his townspeople.

FALL 1961. VANCOUVER

Oh clarity to come,
He played eighteen holes with Lee Mackenzie
and a guy named Mac.

Burnished-head
By burnished-head
they bent over the adequate greens
of the UBC links.

And we ask this—where truth is,
of what use is valour and is worth?

He parred two of the par-threes,
he heard his loan was coming through,

he attends no lectures after Wednesday
of the week, he is a quarter

of a century in age. Later
he will likely know what now

he never dreams of, eyes well focussed
to bear that little white ball

on its dimpled way.

WINTER 1961. VANCOUVER

Amusing & other-
wise, life goes like epi-
sodes, like an idiot
in the face of joy.

He writes an examination
on linguistics.
He records a radio broadcast
with Earle Birney.
He has a scene with one woman
& meets the other.
The other is on the phone saying "that's it"
to her other man.
On his way there he gets his first ever
traffic ticket.
Back in the car he finds it to be
empty of gasoline.
He has to push it half a block to park
uphill.
He has to walk six blocks for gasoline &
six blocks back again.
Later he drives this, his first car,
many many miles, yes
with his hand brake on. He's in love
& losing his girl, & finding
it a little cold, surrounded by Santas
& he's falling in love, & he can
hardly wait to get famous, like a comic strip
in panels.

"SPRING"* 1962. OLIVER

Unable to stop the jangle in his heart,
he carries home from the small familiar post office
two fat letters from his darling today,
three in two days, oh wings,

alas he has them not, not
swift, a bird,
set of God
among the bird-flocks!

Her letters come to him in the desert
from a non-existent place, words
out of nowhere near the green sea.

She barely exists while he loses
these precious summer days away from her,
¡qué lástima!
                    and what an empty sky.

But he is home, and who is this
inside him now, hurting his body inside,
echoing the pain where wings would be?

---

* An error. Instead of Spring, we will get Summer twice.

SUMMER 1962. OLIVER

I have lately been feeling good about being young.
Finished an essay for my poetics book

I'll take years writing. Three fat letters
at the post office, from my "baby," arrive

from a non-existent coast, she exists I guess
while I'm here. He's here. This young poet

country newspaper man, loses "precious days"
away from her. Meanwhile he reads

a novel by touted James Purdy. This
is what he writes: "he like other young

Americans has an ear for dialogue, but pic-
ayunes away at boring days in a dull life."

Bad enough to live them without knowing.

FALL 1962. VANCOUVER

Inside the strangeness of living
as a young man, with.

With A, they went to see his
soppy hero, nearly jazzman, Sammy
Davis Jr., at the Queen
Elizabeth Theatre. It was very nice
to see him at last, gratifying
to hear him do Frank Sinatra
the white guy.

Snow. C.P.
Snow sees the continent of the rich
pull away from the continent of the poor.

We need, he says, to revampire
western education, supply money, send
men to poor lands, prod
their revolutions. China, 1949.

But intellectuals. They are rooted
in the so far
all right soil of the past. They do impressions
(if you want unity) of the past. This
is tradition. Not the strange.

WINTER 1962. VANCOUVER

Al Purdy writes and he's never met him,
pronouns sliding all over the personal,
he says profuse thank-yous for my work
to bring him here
                                        for what
will be war, & I a victim, no
there's no way I'd know that yet.

He does, I do, enjoy all this
widening circle of world, letters falling
from fingers widened far from here.

I thought of a cocktail party today,
my circle of friends never in the city,
my new wife at work, all this

writing with Purdy, McFadden, O Broin.
Here in the city he never hears a word
about poetry. If there is a muse

she must have a postal address.

SPRING 1963. VANCOUVER

She and he had some *hermosa* time tonight,
new frontiers in geography and extremes
in before dinner in-
terim.

More than compensates for fear and tension,
this healthy cinema for supper.

Being in love, he thinks, with a girl
you have liberty to live with all night and day,
is better than being in anything else.

SUMMER 1963. VANCOUVER

Am I the god?
or does this fire carve me
for its use?

The romantic poet falls back on intensity of feeling
rather than striving for clarity & precision.

He lies in bed till the jangling is gone from his head,
then rises and begins a poem by natural light.

He doesnt believe that man is a super creature
exalting his soul over a world made of things
transformed by the superior imagination.

•

A man is more interesting
than man.

Neither is true, both sound swell,
god and fire.

He loves the bush,
not the voice in the bush.

FALL 1963. CALGARY

Five miles to midnight
it is better to taste of frost—
the exquisite frost—
than of wadding and of dead grass.

Trying to be suspenseful,
the lead players skulked around the city
looking guilty enough for an infant
to suspect. Wadding in the script

brought midnight no nearer,
Paris no closer, murder
no colder. No heart
beats in that dull garden.

It is better to taste of Alberta frost
than the servings of Anatole
Litvak.

WINTER 1963. OLIVER

Pry apart the timid souls,
he said, driving 450 miles

of frozen roads, the Rockies
behind them now, A

weeping for the young dog
dead at the vet's, a likely

incompetent. Here the new
puppies help her, and here

family banality and snow, what
a relief, calamity beyond belief.

But tobagganing on the old
golf course, his father behind,

they set a record pace, and jumped
into somersault, into snow crash,

Dad flying over him, fetched
his ear a wallop with his boot,

the other people laughing their
heads off at the top of the hill.

SPRING 1964. CALGARY

Not a doer but an observer, inside
in-sane wrigglings of the night before—

strained isolate earlier today after
fourteen hours of sleep, safe away,

standing in kitchen reading Fitzgerald notes
in New Directions book, or was that also

last night, tycoon of snow, at silent
normally tasty dinner, below zero

wind outside. He shovelled snow in
white blindness, sex organs no longer

a-perk, slyly reading, a book on the bed,
a book on the kitchen table, magazine

on the couch, an artbook on the
coffee table. He goes from one to

another, an architect of the day, a maze
in Christian underworld, also silent!

of aeons ago, outside himself silent.

SUMMER 1964. MÉXICO

He saw his first rhino
in Chapultepec Park, old Aztec
forest.
                    Bruckner's Second Symphony
and Maximiliano's last palace,
                                        never quite
been in Europe, he,
                                            sits on a hill of trees
and sees all México City, all Carlota.

Max in Mex would die, never
go back to Trieste.

                                        you dwell in your father's house,
                                        the gold-wrought porches of Zeus,
                                        apart in the depth of space.

2.

                            Bent old Yanquis with newspapers
sit in Cuernavaca's three squares,
                                                        persistent
boys with Chiclets harass the newcomers,

a lovely park surrounded by wall-spilled *buganvilla*
lies green, waits for afternoon rain
to clean the dust, make a green place
for a strange African animal.

FALL 1964. CALGARY

University of B.C. lecturer Lionel Kearns
has been awarded, this is the only way,
a Canada Council Scholarship, a Canadian poet,
to study at London School, can get his picture,
of Oriental Studies, in the paper.

If there are connections, dont make them.
Got a letter from Lionel today, I guess
you could say he's my best friend.

He's in England now that Fall is here,
after a great mustache in Cuba, drear
visit to Trinidad, multi-racist Island,
Island, Island, Lionel
is spending all his time on Islands,
connections made by airports.

The Canada Council has just announced
it wants to keep our students at home;
our poets can go to Hell, where
no man is a connection.

WINTER 1964. TORONTO

Veracruz about as far east as Winnipeg,
A took her first subway ride,
she's an oven
unlighted.

Saw Harold Town's *Enigmas,* this is truly
the big city his country
is capable of. Veracruz is a kind of Marseille
filled with brown people,
heavy birds on the roof, no snow,
and saw a collection of Op-type
            social oil statements by that famous
            Vancouver painter, what's
            his name?

Veracruz is southwest of here, Hart Crane dead,
they walked wet pavement of Bloor Street
looking at stylish,
looking at what they dont have in Alberta,
say,
a mist in the December air, a taffrail,
a song played on a beach,
a poet having a poet to dinner,
wives happily there.

SPRING 1965. OLIVER

He thinks he could play
good golf if he played
all the time. He could
quit smoking, waste

no time at all.
He and Tony went round
with Mom and Dad.
It was warm, or

what they call here
in the South Okanagan
cold;

leave the stark core
of the rose
to perish on the branch.

SUMMER 1965. OLIVER

She suspects an infant
starts to grow inside them,

while outside her sister calls
for a beauty in this valley.

Only in moments of cricket
or horizon does it appeal to him.

But a baby now. Holding
his sister's baby, he let her appeal

a little, to him.

FALL 1965. CALGARY

He doesnt know what to do about his dog
Frank's new habit of pissing on people.

Today he tried to piss on Tony
but only got the couch.

Then while he was whacking him
his other dog Small got so scared

he emptied his bladder on the mattress.
Then Frank pissed on the floor.

And he, stumbling, kicked over their water dish.

He should forget animal order
and concentrate on his stamp album

but he's run out of hinges.

WINTER 1965. VANCOUVER

Despite this it'll be ghastly at the end,
but now he walks in cotton pants, denim shirt,
feels free in the Coast clime,

saw Moan Collins, old Moan, did the fucking
shopping, went and saw Mike Rice, old
painter, saw Glad-Eyes for a moment,

old Keep-a-Movin' is in California, damn
the routed vocables, others are dead, Warren
of the Introduction is out for dinner,

see him tomorrow when he's tamer, these
Coast people wearing secret names from his books,
cant see him, he's invisible in their pages.

And here he's accused of taking "another
pen of mine." But here it says black medium,
has his own teeth marks on the end. So he

drinks his li'l orange joose and vodka, you bet.

SPRING 1966. CALGARY

It's supposed to be
the beginning of spring.

Eternal concerns vex and charm
the human image, such as

Paul Newman! The left-handed
gun boy, Billy, his strivings

are dust. He, the movie viewer,
supports one George Stevens,

he says American movies, dont
deride them, they are as good

as her European films. Winter
is supposed to be gone, some

of his best friends are American
movie personalities.

SUMMER 1966. DÜSSELDORF

A lame duck last day in Europe
first time, six weeks in a Bug
now packaged for a ship.

                                        Tomorrow
if he's lucky the DC-7 will stay up
eighteen hours, a silver crate
with Pacific on its skin over North
Atlantic, filled with busybody German
Canadians and yowling babes in hammocks,
the classical event that makes
a family of us all.

Waiting for tomorrow and Amerigo,
he blows bubbles, good Bazooka pink
he got for ten *Pfennige* in a machine
on the Krautish street. He cant read
the wrapper comics, she

hates it when he buys gum,
waits for him in that other continent
heart.

FALL 1966. TORONTO

Il faut se rendre, it is moist and windy
after that sunny automobile highway from the west.

He sees Earle as always, wheeling, dealing, weighing
university offers, women, writing, a hot car,
speaking, as they say, engagements.

He has an odd feeling of discontent or unbalance,
walking around in prose. No emotion endures.

Last night he met them all at last,
Toronto bards, they had to be,
Rosy Joe and sweet bp.

In a few days he has to find a house,
domestic lout in a new town, iambic.

He gives up, gives up the thought of giving up,
prose exuded from his ears, sidewalks defiled.

He spends five dollars for four white pills
for a small dog who loves poetry and meat.

WINTER 1966. LONDON

More and more the poets
get their pictures in the papers.

He doesnt know whether that means our world
is getting better

or falling apart. We have no home
save sickness,

a cold coming, a second
between fire and fire.

SPRING 1967. LONDON

Snowing and melting, central
Canaday is March, time to read, he said,
the Fried North Throwup poets, Le
Pang! , Mac
Person! , James Rain
Man! , but hey, this one's pretty
good!

Time, he said, to go to the
York!, sit in on
drums! with the Nihilist Spasm
Band!
                    Yor k-no good,
they said, keep slipping
into time.

                                    And away
to another bar where two drunken men
walk into the women's toilet.

And outside in Ontario
it is snowing out the night sky,
you should be home
standing in right field.

Poem? You can
finish it

[   ]

SUMMER 1967. LONDON

There were literary gents around,
one of them Creeley, he is a friend
& reads a story full of noise
out of a strange little magazine,
laughing, excited. Is this Creeley?

Duncan made him stop, interrupting
time & again till Creeley argued
it's best to quit reading. To quit dream
he woke up.

                                        His wife A
says this is a homosexual story. This day
the humidity is gone, he can walk
to the store quickly, on Oxford Street
at noon, at noon.

FALL 1967. MONTRÉAL

The city feels world exposition
fear, and now a "wildcat"
transit strike, yes, sure,

downtown there are pretty women
hitchhiking in fur coats, long
slow traffic jams. He is

writher in residence going crazy,
a friend's kid pulling Mexican
pots off tables. Too low, fear

of a red-headed kid, he buries
in *The Ginger Man,* light reading,
an easy wing. He regrets nothing.

He thinks of the cities he likes:
San Francisco, México, Istanbul,
Tucson, London,
Vancouver. Here.

WINTER 1967. MONTRÉAL

"He is one of a thousand
non-descript
college types.

He's an observer, not
a doer.

He does not dwell
in his own house.

He has left
the stark core of the rose
to perish on the branch, tough

as petals.

The plot is an old one
with a modern day treatment,

an evening of light reading,
close enough to dry her tears."

SPRING 1968. MONTRÉAL

Curnoe and Fones and he stood in no jazz room
drilling the great Zeppelin mural into place

not place but under-apron path, Dorval
airport, passing Yankee Expo tourists

hauling suitcases full of ironed chinos,
hands stuffed with passports and green dough.

Till the Mounties came their subterranean way
and made them take it down, holes in stone,

all that beautiful Canadian work, take panel
down by panel. Someone had complained

re text, a hand-painted citation from *Freedom*,
re Muhammad Ali and Vietnam. War

Expo, no habitat under concrete. They
departed their tunnel, Cong with art

under arms, a grim angry snort from Greg,
his airship pal, a Canadian walking east,

into U.S. arrivals.

SUMMER 1968. CALGARY

They drove back over the Rockies
to keep his brothers out of jail,
staying five more days till they could
enter their pleas. This late sixties dope scene
playing out its parodic end in Cow Town.

Doubling back; they had just done
their Calgary time, he'd just unpacked
his books and pens in the Okanagan, dogs
running in their parents' yard. Later
travel plans screwed by Calgary. Family?

Well, family. How odd to have brothers
growing up, going to jail. This time
they saw only a glimpse of a bear on
the Trans-Canada. Forked out $75
for Marty's bail, his brothers couldnt find it all.

And he doesnt think that Alan and Heather
are overjoyed to see them back so soon.
And he's got a headache centred in
his left eye.
And they have to drive back, with brothers.

This is how families are formed,
stories are started,
youth is spent.

FALL 1968. MONTRÉAL

The coffee keeps them awake,
the television gets older and older.

He watched in awe plus chagrin
as the Calgary Stampeders clobbered the
Tiger-Cats, aw dam it, in Hamilton.

In Hamilton McFadden sits all night
scrutinizing print, perfect place
for a poet. He's watching with dis-

ease as the Stampeders reach within
seven points of Ottawa. A is
a football widow. He is a Canadian.

There are [tumbleweeds, no] twelve weeks to go till
Christmas holidays, equinox is here,
it is 80 degrees Fahrenheit. In Calgary

it is freeze and snow. They'll never
live there again. He has no poet
to quote. That was "almost intercepted."

WINTER 1968. MONTRÉAL

Eternal concerns vex and charm
our artful lives, headache, stuffy
nose, sore limbs, work on
radio tapes suspended, Curnoe
is here to finish the airport mural
but the propeller motors are stolen,
no tape recorders are available,
they dont even consider the season,
when Tony arrives, headache,
stuffed sinuses, sore legs, New York
in a few days, she is in bed
coughing, the painter & the poet
and the prairie friend do last minute
shopping, while around the only moon
turn Anders and Borman and Lovell,
looking back at us, look at the big blue.

SPRING 1969. WOLFVILLE

A short-hair kid with a Fiat sports car
drove him there, sixty miles

to the faculty club. He smiled as best he could
while a salesman English professor wanted to know

where he could publish his poems. A sociology guy
persuaded him that these apple valley kids

are getting a second-rate education. He drank
as fast as they'd let him, ate as quick as he could.

•

Then, here comes the usual sestet and sentiment:
he remembered animal order, he went home to play

crokinole with Greg Cook's children, *ah,*
squalor was cheated at last, for a bright head

flung back told him when this is over with
we get a late night bed time snack.

SUMMER 1969. TORONTO

Of course the reading in the stadium fell through,
but of course McClelland & Stewart paid his
train fare. Of course the festival is hype, some
business people and a football field, a person
named Eaton and a person named Walker. Said of
course Coach House and Rochdale couldnt put
up a booth, might sell some books and magazines.

That big crowd
was not enlightened
not charming
nor even friendly,
not even to the musicians.

Victor says
that's Toronto at the end of the sixties.

So they got their counterfeit tickets and listened:
The Velvet Underground, Johnny Winter, Procol
Harum. Enjoying the images, jumping
off the train.

All those writers and poets
trying to forgive, trying not
to lord it over those popular celebrities,
eh, Barrie? People wearing velvet
at midsummer, even the colour
wrong.

FALL 1969. MONTRÉAL

He let her appeal, a little,
to him,

            a curious peril, this—
the gods have invented
curious torture for us.

They exhaust her, who brought
as always her novel for them,

consulting. Of their marriage
she is always ready to talk,

and he does,
            about himself, too.

and he hears her buzzing voice
describe his choice.

WINTER 1969. MONTRÉAL

"The seed planted by Kerouac
and tended by Kerouac and others
is now bearing fruit,
and although B isn't rich and famous,
hasn't sold any scripts to Hollywood,
he's doing what he wants and knows
he'll be remembered for it."

—David McFadden

Nineteen years later he's tending
to forget him already,

this Bowerbird in a fruit tree;
he dropped a seed a minute

as our winged friends tend to do,
and whoever cares, oh

axe that tree, bring that bird
to me.

SPRING 1970. MONTRÉAL

Her buzzing voice
enters the forest
where she looks so hard
to see spooks
she doesnt find myth.

Though we wander about,
find no honey of flowers in this waste,
is our task the less sweet?

The lady talks about the
data of her life,
stepping off the boat, facing
the real forest.

Through the forest the keen eye
can see the ground cleared
for the U of T.

SUMMER 1970. MONTRÉAL

The same sorry rut
not between
                        peaches filled with honey
but before the day's television

though he ground out four and a half pages
on jazz and the short poem.

you dwell in your father's house—

He filled out a form for *Who's Who,*
his shortest fiction so far,

though he smoked a cigar with a plastic tip
and got the titles of his volumes correct,

bibliographer.

FALL 1970. MONTRÉAL

Your fellow wretches
will crowd to the entrance—
be first at the gate.

They went over to
their semi-friends', they saw
their recent baby, as ugly
as most.

She suspects
an infant crowds them or will.
Their semi-friend has fancied
up his house;

he must owe someone
thousands of dollars.

WINTER 1970. MONTRÉAL

She does not dwell in her father's house.
She "received" news of his death
last night. First at the gate

then in her heart,
broken and deep
hurt behind her Christmas tree.

Her sister watching his badly behaved body
disappear, husband broke, brothers
adamant, an independent clause
at her wits' end, history in frozen
Island ground.

Their friend's letter pops through the slot.
He wonders what will ruin their Yule
this year. Can she, can she
grin when he gets here? Her own house?

SPRING 1971. OLIVER

Horsing around like a man, he grew excited
driving into the Valley, Valley folk
love capital Vees, Tenney in the car,
out of the car, they can walk
without coats, a little ice on the lakes.

Home was never sickness as other places
were, yesterday they all looked
at his grade two house in Greenwood, fresh
bushes behind it. Here he meets his
sister-in-law and niece, one of whom

promptly and silently pees in his lap.
His dad went curling and he observed,
and then placed Tenney on the midnight bus.
It is plainly ordinary in his mountain
fastness, he walked to his brother's place

giving thought to buying a pre-fab house.

SUMMER 1971. VANCOUVER

A's in the kitchen,
she's an oven,
making baby cake.

This is a commune
he's out of,
at Simon Fraser University
looking for a job.

Fred and Pauline are here
making old connections.

He gave a paper to the profs,
rain, a class to the students,
a straight line to poor sick ears.

no

He wants to bring up this body in
Vancouver,
but does he need a job in that ill place?
ball

He stokes the stove,
practice he averts the gaze,
he takes his turn
on cooking days.

FALL 1971. VANCOUVER

Keep slipping into time, tomorrow
the baby's due, they have at
last a first
name, Thea, because all the dreams
say it's a girl, she's an it
self.
          Today his new book arrived, its name
is *Touch*, of course,
                              and Tenney said
looks like you've got the job, everything
happens at once, and that isnt the
½ of it.
            D brought some hash
and a knitted shawl for the bairn,
why knot?
                Dont, said D, get
excited, wrap yourself in this
smoke.
           They worked on his
manuscript, of course, bring a book
into the world,
                         a job can wait
till all this is begun.

WINTER 1971. VANCOUVER

Before he left Lawrence this time he was rooting around in the cellar, looking for a brick or a two-by-four to go with his baby, and he saw a vertical cubbyhole where he used to keep his collection of broken baseball bats. It came to his mind that he might remember stashing something there when he was a kid. He dipped his arm through the spiderwebs and came up with his October 1947 *Sunbathing for Health* magazine. He remembered every archer and every beach ball nude, all the grey photos he had looked at so often, their air-brushed genitals. Inside the magazine was his 1946–1947 certificate that proved he was a junior Maple Leafs fan. His father had been a Canadiens fan. His father knew it said affiliated, but he had a good laugh when his son read aloud: officially afflicted with the Toronto Maple Leafs. Slipping *out* of time, too.

SPRING 1972. VANCOUVER

He's had Bruckner's
third symphony out of the jacket
for days, but never
gets the chance to play it.

Weed, moss-weed,
root tangled in sand,
puddles at shortstop
make his footing something

other than baseball.
He and his mother took Gumpy
for a long walk in the buggy.

He hardly saw his mother and daughter,
but rather Honus Wagner at short,
a devout music of stumpy flesh.

SUMMER 1972. VANCOUVER

He begins to despair of seeing
serious critics in his life
time for his life's
work.
            The reviewers chase after
a major writer among old hacks
back east, or coo excitedly
after a personality.
                                        Oh, depend on it,
he writes of serious, maybe eternal
concerns that vex and charm
the human mind, but no commentator
notices.
              They cluck over the subject
of the apparent state of his emotions.

One might as well despair
or pose for front porch snapshots
with the Greeks across the street.

If it looks as if nothing will develop,
get together again, take another,
that's the Greek way. Regret nothing.

FALL 1972. VANCOUVER

He asked Joseph Brodsky
what's the difference between the Leningrad poets
and the Moscow poets.

                                        The baby had
fallen down the stairs her first time,
old tears round her eyes.

                                            They are
more sophisticated, the Leningrad poets,
in the good sense, he replied.

                                              The poet
Lionel Kearns bent over his plate, finished
his pie while his friend was half way
through his salad.

                                    The woman
from the Russian Department surrounds
the Leningrad poet with deans and
chairpersons.

                              Separated by a table,
the Vancouver poets bent their heads
and ate, some more politely than others.

WINTER 1972. VANCOUVER

The bills unpaid, un-
payable, the cheques written
cannot be mailed, the bank
is empty, the poor little tree
is atop a stereo speaker,
the new dishwasher gleams.

Was Whitman right? Should he
dance? He has a pain
behind his left eye, they
have no sickness save home
but a child separated from a tree
by a chair. They

save her from pulling it over
on herself, she who
never sits anyway. Was
Duncan right? He makes a poem
ending with a word called Pindar.

SPRING 1973. BURNABY

"He has consistently amazed Canadians with his poetic ineptitude and public relations ability.

"I felt sad that a grown man could stand up there and make such an ass of himself, displaying his lack of intellect and invisible technique.

"His poems are for the most part strung-out, contorted, awkward, and generally fucked-up.

"B and his crew are body stealers, scrounging on the scraps and remains of their predecessors, milking what they can from their betters.

"I have heard incredible visions and perceptions of the visible and invisible world from half-crazed anarchist loggers.

"There is a need for such conversation between the community of poets."

—B.T. Brett

SUMMER 1973. VANCOUVER

Why learn to speak at all?
If only to enter a stupid dispute
with a crazed poet in a redneck magazine?

Why not quietly produce a new book
and call him your old pal,
make up a life together?

Life with him was always
like that, a barrel of sobs, a
red face and a red face, a

squirrel on a bird-feeder, a
dodging of libel, hey, Miltie,
I loved your poem about Lycidas,

I thought that was a good drug,
keeps you forgetting the great war
and the great failure at war.

Soon a painter will show up,
come round, drop over, fall by,
make a brush with greatness,

put an end to speech.

FALL 1973. VANCOUVER

He worked diligently along the beach,
raking piles of human eyeballs.

He took the first copy
of Warren's little booklet over today,
his first separate publication.

Warren went to another room
for a hanky. "Honk!"
What's that? asked the child.

She's nearly two. That's
my house, she said earlier.
"That's, ah, wonderful," said Warren.

Life with her
                    was always like this.

WINTER 1973. VANCOUVER

No drinks, no polished wood,
and no one will ever know

whether the picture he saw clearly
as in a mirror included a child

or only old age. She came home hot
from the daycare, had no real supper,

she asked to go to bed at six. She
had a little nosebleed at the party

and now looked funny round the eyes.
All day at the party the big kid Jordan

knocked her off things. Why learn to speak
and then have only ill health to say?

He looked into the future, and all he saw
was gold, frankincense, myrrh, soil.

SPRING 1974. VANCOUVER

Brian won the first game of snooker
and he came second.

will you fling your spear-head
on the shore?

Dwight won the second game
and he tied for second.

I break a staff.

Brian won the third game
and he tied for second.

I break the tough branch.

Then they played a bunch of poker pool
and when it was over Dwight came first
and he came second.

I know no light in the woods.
I have lost pace with the wind.

SUMMER 1974. VANCOUVER

Daphne called, the Bau-Xi Gallery
is on fire, the whole block
is smoke & red light.

The kid isnt three, someone
has to watch her while her mother
takes a warm bath for her shrink.

We have to save the paintings—
Boy! fifty miles an hour down 41st,
leave the kid with Grandma

then fifty miles an hour the opposite direction,
there, thigh-deep in freezing water,
hauling out paintings by Roy and others

in that clear place
where the women dip
their water-jars,

no time to reflect on the death of art.
When he brings hours later a painting home,
he has to hang it in his room

away from the anger, go get the kid,
figure out dinner.

FALL 1974. VANCOUVER

It is 80 degrees Fahrenheit. In
Vancouver
the Granville Grange Zephyrs beat
the Flying Dildos 24–19. Post-season
baseball as lovely as having

a daughter nearly three. They had together
the mom, the game, Queen Elizabeth
Park, a visit to Dwight's place,
five new kittens. Be careful, he said

like an idiot in the face of joy.
He and Dwight proofread the last pages
of an anthology, what a Sunday, warm
as a new feline belly. He watched

in awe as well as chagrin. What
a stupid dad, be really careful, he
cautioned. Cautious. A caution. A cat
might get you, a line drive

might break your cheekbone ten years
from now. Look out. Dwight
is a poet he once shamelessly quoted,
no, stole from.

WINTER 1974. VANCOUVER

This is tradition,
not the strange.
She makes good use
of the *NY Times* cookbook he got
as introduction to that book club. He's
getting a belly

full. "B
reveals that it's easier to write
poems about nothing than it is to write
short stories about nothing."

Ian Dunn died on the highway
ten years ago, his funeral last night
occurred in a cave. When he was
carried in I saw his head bobbing.
Etc.

Little Gumpy,
with her small stem glass,
has become something of an expert
wine fancier,

a short story becoming more familiar
with time.

SPRING 1975. VANCOUVER

Her buzzing voice,
almost, this afternoon,
talks about writing,

Peggy, he didnt say
what you say he said,
he didnt have it in his head,

but he is happy to see you
listen. To get some
of the attention.

We forgot—for a moment
tree-resin, tree-bark,
sweat of torn branch
were sweet to the taste.

SUMMER 1975. VANCOUVER

The day he went two for three
his friend Tenney tried to sell
a three-wheeled motorcycle, closed in,
a steering wheel for steering,

a bad idea, said Tenney, asking
$250, if you're heading for a
collision, the other driver
doesnt know your intention.

And he was put out, nervous now,
he was trying to sell a motorcycle too,
made two errors at short,
laid down a perfect bunt,

making up a life together.

FALL 1975. VANCOUVER

Not a deer but an observer, wangled
a free pass to the novelist show at UBC,

bearer of a .298 batting average, sat down
for free lunch. Six hundred people and he

is the last to get his roast beef, piled
other people's roast potatoes on his plate.

The mid-seventies fiction life, playing ball
on teams with silly names, blowing the relay,

routing the vocables, charms him while
he seems to sleep. Peggy A comes over again,

says she hopes she's pregnant, kid wont
play ball in 2015 AD. Robert K looks

good, maybe grey. Audrey T managing
humour. There's a blonde trash novelist

tries to stay sexy in boutique clothes,
says she's an awetist.
He gets roast beef

at gigs like this, wrote a novel once,
gave it a serious name.

WINTER 1975. VANCOUVER

All these visits when the earth seems
to tilt away,
                    now, for instance, in Cuba,
we are all in green or brown fatigues
and the sun is down, we
simply lie on the ground, young
men and women, to sleep.

Strength.
To endure.

But in the small university classroom
a middle-aged female professor
and a middle-aged male professor
urge their sociology on us,
standing up clean, big clean eyeglasses.
Explaining the young revolutionaries.

Buy.
That makes him mad.

He'd rather lose something
and slowly come to realize
it's gone.

SPRING 1976. VANCOUVER

She's watching *The Red Shoes,*
getting educated on PBS, while he

remembers his boring childhood, no
Winnie-the-Pooh, no Alice

in Wonderland. But A,
who remembers everything, says

this movie gets ghastly at the end,
she did read him Winnie and Alice, that

was their honeymoon, he says
I'll take her out for an hour

before the hockey game, his boring
adulthood, except for this, this

having a future, getting educated,
stepping off the boat, facing the real

forest or the Washington Capitals.

SUMMER 1976. VANCOUVER

How does he know it'll be ghastly
at the end? At the front door
of their cottage he saw the door knob
explode, then was inside
a roaring. His body figured out
he was being shot at from behind.
A never before experienced thing
in the whole right side of his body,
he had no time to get inside, now
the strangeness of dying, what form,
no help, he tried to call for help
but his voice is a whisper. Awake
in bed he whispers for help but A
in the next room cannot hear him,
he cannot move to see. He is awake
and dying, they did not require of him
that he keep a day free.

FALL 1976. VANCOUVER

Island, Island, I wish I were no man.
In the basement, doing laundry,
in the kitchen, doing supper,
in the lineup, buying canned goods,
four-year-old at the table.

2:45, Mom leaves for dinner groceries
again; 7:30, others go for hamburgers
again; 12:45 a.m., Mom comes home
again, cant walk straight.

                                        One day
Mom tried to cook supper, couldnt make the spaghetti sauce
work. What's wrong, Mom, says
four-year-old at the table with crayons;
Mom says to Dad, very loud, "If your fucking
friend tries to give us another of these,
he can shove it up his ass." Four-year-old
looks downward.

                                        Does she think
this is normal in a kitchen? Does she know
Mom wishes she were cooking elsewhere?

He wishes he was at most an isthmus,
a continental compromise.

WINTER 1976. VANCOUVER

Telling the truth under the raindrops
on a walkie-talkie,
                                        dream of his
childhood, he knew as unattainable.

                                  He was familiar
with unattainable then, now
                                              he has
a daughter who claims it'll snow
for Christmas.

                                   He's giving her
a magic talking machine, after all,
how to live in this world
where they get what they want.

              His best ever Christmas day was
1971, his daughter was two months old.

                    His worst year ever
was this one.

                              He's talking to himself
again, he's walking in circles.

SPRING 1977. VANCOUVER

He and Curnoe sat in the new jazz room
filled with the Art Ensemble of Chicago.

They didnt care how long it was, this
wonderful music in their whole systems.

Overjoyed, overjoyed, his living friend
here on the coast, these wonderful black men

before them, unbelievable instruments of sweet
torture scattered on the floor by their feat,

scary as an outdoor elevator, Greg sitting
behind his mustache, what snug harbour,

what skyway, what trumpet to those
angelic Illinois lips. You go out, you climb up,

and love is louder than you had imagined,
favors ricochet from the walls, Curnoe

is wearing stripes and they vibrate, the streets
may be filled with smoke, sirens burn down,

music whispers to the node in the centre of his brain,
speech will have to wait.

SUMMER 1977. VANCOUVER

His mother and his auntie
gone to Ketchikan
with Captain
Van-
couver.

New frontiers in someone's geography,

but gee,
his other half is loud
reciting all his wrongs
in fifteen years,
                                        exploration
an easy trope, a tropic
trick,
                 they have disagreed
about coffee again.

                                                 She never, she says,
attacked him with scissors or knife,
not in her life
this wife.

FALL 1977. VANCOUVER

David Robinson was over last night
with blue line of his book,
with cover mock-up, with
long eye lashes, deep brown eyes.

The coffee keeps them awake.
The poems burn them up.

It certainly looks good, but it looks
as if it wont be made in time
for his October reading tour, not in time
to go to Europe with it in his hand.

This long disease my life
is much the same this year.

Romantic, at last, he may never see
that book, but if the plane crashes
nobody'll ever read these words either.
Oh how I love it!

WINTER 1977. VANCOUVER

If there are no connections, dont make them.
Supervise the little kids, rooms familiar to all,

the great cement complex, sore throat, a care.
The first room is a giant pinball machine,

kids spread around its edge at controls.
He made some beautiful shots, right into

the hole at top. Bells ring. Get bored. Move
room to room, decide which to skip. The kids

come filing, male adults too, dads, wont
look at him, he's accused of abandoning his bunch.

But they're in the pool, T's there. He has to
look downward through windows, she's getting in.

Her rapid dog-paddle is her secret, I'm glad
she's got one, she puts down head, lifts bum

and rises from the chop where she was all the time
going. Her mother is signed up for an abortion,

not many days now. What's in all those cement rooms?

SPRING 1978. VANCOUVER

Feeling fairly good about being
middle-aged.

When he went away in January Dennis Wheeler died, and when he went away in March Russell Fitzgerald died. Both deaths were expected, but both were cruel to us all and especially to them. He thinks death is worse for the dying than for the survivors, though people act as if the opposite were true. Anyway it is almost that he's loath to go away again to return to the fact of another friend's death, though the one he fears most is his own during these plane trips.

"What stands out is the impossibility of resistance one feels in reading these poems, however unpalatable their content."

—Bruce Whiteman

SUMMER 1978. VANCOUVER

Yesterday they had lunch with the poet.
This was just before his reading.

T has four more days of Grade One.
He has lately been feeling bad about getting old.

If they were an art gallery
they'd be on fire.

He and the poet were friendly as always.
He likes him save for one thing.

He is glad too that T is still so young.
Looking ahead with misgiving. Tender wings.

Any symphony by Bruckner, played loud enough
will please you if you're just starting middle age.

If he just didnt have this terrific desire
to be taken seriously. But I sympathize too.

At lunch he didnt have time to eat everything.
There was hardly anyone at his reading.

FALL 1978. VANCOUVER

At a tryout camp for football team
we late arrivals were handed, we who were
not expected to make it were handed
not football uniforms but priest robes,
dressing gowns, sharp white shins.

There were literary gents around, the coach
told him to stick his body into the rush,
frightened, a hard back-hand clout
to his windpipe. He sends no
string of pearls.

                                        The regulars without
shoulder pads, with large numbers, black
red & white, dark, huge arms.
There would be no padding
in his robe, little vocation, he was late
dressing
                    as when he got fired up north,
from the survey gang. He said you did this
last year, B, failure.

He ran up the stairs, his shoes
in his left hand.

WINTER 1978. KALEDEN

He washed and dried her hair and now
she looks gorgeous,

a seven year old daughter,
Okanagan light through blonde;

she got off the Greyhound,
a suitcase in her hand,
her back straight,
pure food in her stomach,
no buzz in her voice.

The Dutch in front of them
were thankful to have seen
mountains full of snow,
a road black tires make
every minute of the way.

Here over this dark lake
the dainty dogs scamper indoors,

the little girl waits
till they bound into her lap.

SPRING 1979. VANCOUVER

She allowed him as promised
to take her to the small perfect
French restaurant.

After they got home she
pursued her lad
                                        on the phone,

a sound in the dark air of this cave
when the flame is low & tidy,

and now what is it that has come to pass?
for fire has shaken my hand,
my strivings are dust.

                                                    He lay in bed
unable to stop
                                        the jangle
in his brain.

                                        Unable to read
the menu in the flickering light.

SUMMER 1979. VANCOUVER

He went to the Cecil after work
    to drink a dream, drop a poem—

dreamt they promoted him to full
    professor, oh no, an academic fancy

only, said Jack, furniture in the room,
    like anything else, said this shortly

before he died, a linguist shut up
    lying under raindrops, the count

was three and oh, and everyone knew
    he was coming in with his fastball.

Fourteen years ago, inconsolable memories,
    that's what we have, in the Cecil

they quote Jack and denigrate the Giants,
    truly reflexive and intelligently social.

They dream beer dreams, and drink rue,
    they make pencil notations in the street.

FALL 1979. VANCOUVER

Kroetsch, his beard still
a little black, grinned
while looking into
a copy of *What the Crow*
Said in his left hand.

The widening circle of world
can be traced by feathers
avoiding extra innings, away games
and twin bills.

                                        If it's Friday
I can work for myself, he said,
having heard everything the bird
had to say, calmly putting foot
after foot, pacing out a radius

thus

getting away from the still
centre.

WINTER 1979. VANCOUVER

M got him up this morn
arriving with revised thesis

he must turn in this afternoon,
a circle, the end of a straight line.

He is M's advisor, fellow student,
would collaborate on a novel,

fellow actor, college
journalist, criss-cross, guest lecturer,

universities across the country, growing
older, invitee, on the island.

Throw them into a common grave,
celebrate a post-graduate degree,

open wide the yawking mouths,
pry apart the timid souls.

SPRING 1980. VANCOUVER

"Self-consciously clever
and indulgently obscure,

here is a charmingly irreverent
intellect confused as to how

seriously it should take
life. The arrogantly arid humour

is redeeming; the poet's
inability to get a third erection

is not." He regrets nothing.

Among his favourite cities are
Amsterdam, Sydney, Halifax, here.

SUMMER 1980. VANCOUVER

A notes that he finds
B in his amused terror
my spiritual kin.

It is with fond pleasure
and little of the old bafflement
I follow him to the stretcher,
to the grave, to the earth
a crawling hole. Ha. Ho.

This is not the strange now,
I mean, if meaning is more
than a hoe in the dirt, a ha,
not the strange, and not the
family trade. Oh finally

shoes will be useless save for
feet pointing upward, his best
walking shoes, shining

in the dark. Classical re
duction, makes a family of us all,
even his happy daughter.

FALL 1980. VANCOUVER

Later, they read his bunt,
so he bunted hard
past the charging
pitcher and first, and
the vacating second

for a hit and an RBI.
And under and under,
the wind booms:
it whistles, it thunders,
it growls—it presses the grass

and he binged a triple
off the crossbar
of the goalposts in centre field.

What fun the last day of summer
to play ball with his friends,
Thane, Billy, Jim, James,
Laura, and Bob.

If he can pray
he'll speak their names.

WINTER 1980. COURTENAY

On the deck of the ferry
his daughter stood and then a large
helicopter flew over her, playing
Christmas music, fire
like words bursting from treetops.

Captain, my captain, he skated
with the children, till he essayed
a crossover step, fell on his chin,
lost consciousness, the classical
relation that makes a family of us all.

On the deck nearing Nanaimo
stood Paul with Trudy pregnant,
a bit dizzy, non-smokers
and friends, his daughter

as far as possible from the poor old woman
having a heart attack in the sea-going
painted women's head. On the slip
the ambulance flashes, as he lies on the ice
his personal stars give way, rotor blades
confuse time, and they are there at last,
he is sitting now, hoping
no one skates over his glasses.

SPRING 1981. MONTRÉAL

He from one side,
I from the other,
converged on the same slender vase,

the best piece of glass
in the narrow shop.

There was also
a beautiful woman from Sweden.

Later he gave me his first edition
Williams, good Lord—

I send no string of pearls,
no bracelet—accept this

taken poem
to be our own.

SUMMER 1981. VANCOUVER

~~There, over that dark sea~~
~~the dainty *Doge* has scampered indoors.~~

Love the world and stay inside it
a gently eccentric and not uninteresting personality,

the kinky cranky observer who is happy merely,
more gnarly and complex than he is sometimes

willing to let on, a man on a horse,
a man with a gun. A combination of humour

plus sense embodies the mute anger and
the ill foe surrender of a man speaking.

FALL 1981. VANCOUVER

Seeing that he's reading books by *B*'s,
he can sample
Samuel Beckett, gorge on
Jorge Luis Borges, nibble
Nicole Brossard.

Burnished-head
By burnished-head,
Pierides sought the bride:
They touched the flute-stops
And the lyre-strings for the dance,

while he turns over
Adolfo Bioy Casares, adjusts to
Djuna Barnes, he smiles as best he can
while an English professor lectures on John Bunyan.

Now that he's going through the *B*s,
he can take
Bryher to his bed,
he can seek a bride in Emily
Brontë, that burnished head.
The alphabet
settles by a low river, dark around light tents,

where the dance begins, his favourite partner is
Charlotte, and he may never have another,

oh Adam long gone, oh Clarity to come.

WINTER 1981. VENICE

Here beside this dark sea
the dainty *Doge* has scrambled indoors.

How lucky they were yesterday
to see snow in St Mark's Square,

how lucky today to look out their window
on people in hip waders
carrying widows across the riva.

At five-thirty in the morning
he woke to hear Italian shouted below,

from mature throats. Yesterday in the Basilica
the children's choir faltered
when the parents' applause
greeted the Cardinal's entrance from offstage.

Later outside, the liberated boys and girls
were learning to make snowballs.

This, he told his daughter,
is what happens when you marry the sea.

SPRING 1982. MÉXICO

Today he said to himself
how can you be said to be enjoying yourself
when you are in endless pain?

He hobbled from gallery to gallery.
His backbone broken like an Aztec pot
if you need a colourful local metaphor.

At Galería Pecanins the Cuevas exhibition
was closed, at the Gallery of Modern Art
Riopelle, Guston, & Cartier-Bresson
cerrada.

            He enjoys this widening circle
of world, his back is shattered, the smog
chases him into Vips for lunch, the best
guacamole this side of Portland, Oregon.

He is enjoying himself, he loves travel,
he is very happy to be alone, he
is glad he can still stand in the street.

SUMMER 1982. VANCOUVER

This is family tradition,
not the strange.
                                        He went
to the shopping centre, wanting
to buy himself something, came home
with new sneakers for his daughter.

She came home from school,
ten years old, started
to write a book, ah God,
wrote from 3:30 till 10:00 p.m.,
twenty minutes for piano, wrote
while she ate her late supper,

never showed what the book would be.
Crippled Feo, the lovely cat
has one front paw and her face
in the hidden swallow's nest,
suddenly healthy sneak.

                                                            She,
the girl, may and may not
wear the shoes tomorrow, her father
too busy to write for a decade,
too plain for reward.

FALL 1982. VANCOUVER

He does not dwell
in his own house,
cannot clean his daughter's room.
                                                            Will she
                                                            frown at
                                                            a stranger,
                                                            ride her bike,
                                                            her mind
                                                            countries afar?

Electricians in every room, grinding
at something, drywallers yesterday, plumbers
tomorrow,
                    his word processor
in a protective box for eight days
already.

                It will never be free,

a house is not a home but a house.
A life will never be lived.

                                              His daughter
will inherit, owing a million dollars.

He breaks no staff.
He breaks no tough branch.

He knows no light
in the woods.

WINTER 1982. VANCOUVER

Home was never sickness but now
he has no home save in dreams,

in which a very pretty woman shows
pictures of bpNichol who was her

husband, comic-strip maker in which
he the dreamer makes words

play, 1979, tansy in all the pages,
iambs in morpho-land, the name

the [something] *Muse.* He dreams
more panels, sick for home, in which

an old friend who does not remember
tells of a discussion concerning

whether he is there.

SPRING 1983. VANCOUVER

Last night in Camrose an elevated sign
by the highway into town
bore Rudy Wiebe's name and his
in lights.

They never did that for him in L.A.!

Does the fire carve him for its use?
He flew back here today with the Detroit Red Wings,
traded words with Danny Gare and Ivan Boldirev.

So you have swept me back,
I who could have walked with the live souls
above the earth.

Over Vancouver a little girl in prairie clothes
said, "Mummy, look at the big green!"

SUMMER 1983. VANCOUVER

He marked one paper
this morning, wrote desultory letters,
typed two chapters of
Craft Slices,

you will come,
you will answer our taut hearts,

had lunch at Mr. Roberts,
cleaned up garbage pails,
put away his fragrant laundry,
drove the car through the safety test,

bodies are falling from the sky,
bombs know no one,

visited Celia's remainder store,
looking forward to sitting down
in front of the Expos
game.

FALL 1983. OLIVER

Home town is the still
centre he's been getting away from
all these widening circles, these

men, John the director and
Doug the camera man and somebody
younger the sound man.

Roy the friend the consultant
and Pearl the mom. A simple
little movie, the orchard, the

ballpark, the dried mud, the
late slanting sunlight, the nouns
a little place is made of. A kid

never did come back to be filmed,
just this middle-aged man, all
excited, as if *he* were the kid,

as if he had brought those
tender stinking wings
to earth.

WINTER 1983. VANCOUVER

It's like pants that feel sticky in the middle,
this mulligan stew. You dont care

how long it is, not so hard to get into
as you'd expected, you just like being

inside it. Autographs on a cup beside you,
smoke in your whole system, the first

blood clot in your leg, ten years later where
you're outside it. Not quite halfway through

if it's a book, a long way past the middle
if it's a life. Float on a joke

and go under again, whoever made this, him
and whose army? You'd like to join. But

he's in another country and another before that
and he doesnt give a shit about you. You're

neither going to make a high water mark,
you come back to this from time to time,

in your pants too long, could at least
have stayed out of the chowder.

SPRING 1984. TORONTO/VANCOUVER

In the fireplace room at Ithaca
where there was church there was

Curious, friends to see in Ontario,
fuel to pump into wings,

metric measure to remember. Sarah
insisted on spelling her name Saraht

because she loves *T* as her father
adores *H,* a letter or ladder

to a Higher place. Fire from
these wings? Hope keeping us aloft,

an *H* in the heart, he says smugly,
a daughter to fate, his holding

a chocolate *T* last Christmas, all these
private visits he loves and readers

stand or dont. The craft, to be plain,
looks new, not many riders in it, flying

from snow to know, he cannot kneel
but he adores you, daughters, he wings

on by your inquisitive smiles.

SUMMER 1984. VANCOUVER

There are pieces in the paper,
papers on the street, where

is Kerrisdale? There is lively wit in this
book, without wasting an ounce of

fuel, fully conscious of mortality,
what happened to that smile

that was on your floor an hour ago?
Mud and metaphor, he never would have

said it so smugly, but he thanks
the man, why not? True, she caught

his breath with her fingers; what is
breath? Who lives here? Not the noisy

dog next door late at night. There's
something red under the snow, a

wise woman leaves it there; if she's a poet
she's dead like the rest of them.

Thanks, he says, a long way
under his breath, thanks for the meal.

FALL 1984. VANCOUVER

Riding away into the east,
she denies *comédie* to them,
the shrivelled seeds

are split on the path—
the grass bends with dust.
He didnt have it in his head

to hold him back,
but he held back,
he sat his horse

and watched her ride away.
She is riding to remain
single, to remain a legend
beginning to fade.

WINTER 1984. VANCOUVER

Tender stinking wings—
on the phone a voice says
your poem wins a bunch
of money.

The art gallery's on fire—
at your desk the essay
lies finished, nine thousand words,
seamless, cruel, and long.

Floating over the Alps—
you have three chapters
ready for the fancy
hand-printed signature, congratulate
yourself.

Arrogantly arid humour—
your book has one page to go,
they cant say
you dont use your gift of time.

Last minute shopping—
the world is getting tired of Christmas
almost as fast
as the people who live there.

SPRING 1985. ROME

One flower in the garden of his little hotel,
really a new kitten, he dreamt, skinny

as the woman writing in Italian
of Kroetsch, white it was, with brown splotches,

a flower beaten by rain, unnamed
by this lorn Canadian. Dreamt also

of his orange mother in the verandah bedroom,
young, rising from bed. Toronto birds

would love this March ground, never
find a road here. His cat would

pounce on them, a child sprung
into the world, no foes around.

He said, oh, are you in here? She
smiled on her student horsing about

like a man.

SUMMER 1985. BERLIN

If he can pray
he'll pray for them,

wife and daughter
in skies of slaughter

come to meet him in Germany
while he is in *Suisse*.

Bodies are falling from the sky,
bombs know no one's God.

If he can pray
he'll pray third for me,

floating over Alps
in a USAmerican jet.

FALL 1985. VANCOUVER

Write about the book you
liked or hated reading this summer
he asked them. Boy, are they
dumb! His boring old age
stares him in the face.

Rout the damned vocables, the phone
is Michael O, he's glad
he's going to Rome, he told them
get Mike. He thinks despite this
it'll be ghastly at the end.

Give wing to the deformities,
in Europe he had wide open
frontiers of time, he could read
and write and walk in the world
on sidewalks near sausages.

Goat-foot, not old yet, lonely
for a daughter gone in another
family's car to Cultus Lake, wearing
her new red shoes.

WINTER 1985. VANCOUVER

Doubling back.
Dropping his crisp red copy of *Zazie*
dans le métro face open
in a car-wash puddle.

Dont want any rhythm
to settle into,
like to hear lines of words that step and stop.

Absolutely
not.

But he lifts the book and there
'S a five-year-old inter-
view, he said
                    In Lyric You Look And Say.
                    In Later Long Poems
                            You Listen And Write.

You Be and Ell.

A and T are in the kitchen making
Christmas cake, lots of yelling
going on.

And on.

SPRING 1986. VANCOUVER

First he ate some
Barthes for lunch.

Then he decided numbers
might follow letters.

He ate some Heath
cinema for dinner.

Well over twenty
years of age. Just like that.

He may have done
a number, then left

the remainder for
someone else, perhaps

half-crazed
anarchist loggers.

SUMMER 1986. VANCOUVER

People seem not to follow
the connections he will make.

Playing between raindrops
he took a skipper on the chin.

Looking for a brick or a two-by-four
or a dress he can be Helena
in.

His wife really liked her,
as who doesnt? Roger Clemens

trying to go thirteen and nothing
understands nothing.

There are no connections, one makes
the things that are not connections.

He enjoys doing anything
to get a rally going, a squeeze play,

a dream in the middle of summer,
good food but too much of it.

FALL 1986. VANCOUVER

Classical re-
lation makes a family of us all.

He returned from the field of play
to see after a daughter
and nine nieces, a first
nephew, named as is the fashion
Kevin. And two parents.

    And then two Albanian
communists from North
Vancouver.

He baited them, accused them,
called them idealists, conservatives,
the nineteenth century.
              Their world
is always changing, they
believe in immutable theory,

have no children. His brother
has no politics.

        Kevin and Karl
and he in his baseball duds,
a Sunday like any other.

WINTER 1986. VANCOUVER

Family banality and the phone, what
relief, calamity beyond belief.

They put up
the tree

with it
s normality

for she
is there to see.

He proposed
and put up
or shut up
alternately.

He has never made much
of his feelings. He
wouldnt know how
to answer the question,
never win the prize.

The tree glistens/blisters in their eyes.

SPRING 1987. VANCOUVER

In shirtsleeves at last and
        standing in right field late
in practice he said it is
        this day that makes you glad
you didnt kill yourself
        in December.

The poet Brian Fawcett bent over
        the plate, finished his thought
with an awkward swing, uttered
        a nasty disappointed word
the man in right field
        handled with ease.

SUMMER 1987. VANCOUVER

"The tall vengeance-seeker
is a red-haired woman."

FALL 1987. WHISTLER

Talking to himself again, walking
in circles someone else designed,

they limp, he says, we
have children. See what they are

trying to resemble, while he
breaks into tears in the shower,

clock towers and painted roofs,
crooked roads wide enough for

North American fire trucks. He
imagined his daughter in a coffin,

couldnt get her out of his mind.
Here he had a yup-burger

at a bar called La Cittá, wealthy
young under umbrellas, looking

beautiful. His mind's pictures,
dont deride them, escape

the voice riding him while his tears
flowed down with the rest.

How did he drive the highway to death,
the wipers still in bright sun?

WINTER 1987. TORONTO

Making a life together while
some of them are dying, some,
drifting, a Harry William Bowering
nabbed for assaulting a woman.

Gwen is dead, Stan is bereaved,
just got to know her, looked for
ward, another island gone, bp
is over, eating a plate of cookies.

Earle had a stroke, memory slides
and it's gone. I'm leaving, he says,
on a jet plane, but Paul is over
for chicken and a hockey game on TV.

Frank is alive, but he's leaving soon,
out of town. David introduced him to
his girl, a woman from memory,
surrounded by students of some sort.

There are pieces in the paper.
There are papers in the hall.

SPRING 1988. VANCOUVER

Enjoying the images, jumping off the train.

He and his father are in a Niagara Peninsula
man's orchard, famous white-hair
Ontarian, right now being interviewed
on TV, something important.
                                        He breaks
the tough branch.
                              The trees are short
and filled with enormous ripe peaches
the owner is picking. His father
is after something else, he has permission
providing he leaves the peaches alone.

American movies, dont deride them.

The peaches, says his father,
are like drinking honey.

                                  On the stage
Daphne dances, earlier, earlier, her shirt
rolled at her waist, her very small breasts
bare.

        His father not, then, there.

SUMMER (WINTER) 1988. CANBERRA

He loves them, he loves
being with them, his dear Aussies,
an A in the heart. They care
for each other, they fly from
know to yes.

A long way from home
at the end. It happened that way. A
peacock in the snow would be fine,
a plane crumpled in a forest. Exploded words
catching fire, classical relation
ship in your poem, maybe.

A curious peril,
the gods have in mind, Küsnacht
will look prosperous and lonely, a
woman walking with him will resemble
a ghost.

But here in Canberra it is
midwinter already. They eat outdoors at long tables.
The movie gets ghastly at the end
but it isnt
the end.

Los Pájaros de Tenacatita

La Manzanilla del Mar, Jalisco
January 2013

(Nose-in-Book, 2013)

The *fulcro* (fulcrum) is a verse form I learned from the example of the Cuban American poet Pablo Medina. It can be seen in his bilingual volume *Points of Balance / Puntos de Apoyo* (Four Way Press, 2005). The middle couplet bears a discernible relationship to the first couplet and another to the third couplet, but the third couplet need not be seen or heard in relationship to the first couplet. Pablo Medina said that with the fulcrum he wanted to get both the dialectic of the sonnet and the image of the haiku.

BREATHING IN

White pigeons on the corrugated
church roof, *alas,* they fold

wings beyond his language.
Words arrive on a Brazilian

jet liner, dropping like
spent insects onto his page.

AGE OLD

Laila may be four years old,
the puppy in her hands in front

of her chest, six weeks old.
His old *manos* remember two

Chihuahuas, ignorant of the
life they were always saving.

BLUE HANDKERCHIEF

Watching blue sky *como* Pablo
Medina, he finds an aesthetic

made of frigate birds saying
nothing. Great is their height,

humble is *Jesús* in his passion
along the church's inside walls.

COWS, FISH

Beef Wellington on a rooftop,
punto de apoyo, gringo economy

clear as tomorrow morning's
nets in the sea. Mexicans there

are more beautiful, they are young,
they have children.

HE SETS HIS WATCH

6:20 every night the black and
yellow critters gather in two trees

then pulse in groups of ten
straight at his face and over

his soul if he still has one,
knowing he has never been a bird.

THE COWBOY

It is difficult to seat a woman
in voluminous wedding dress

atop even a patient braided horse
in front of our little *iglesia*.

Where he has never knelt nor
has he crossed himself or swords.

A SILLY RIME

Five Norwegian babes at the beach
have trios of clear assets each

from which he turns his gaze away
to follow the pelicans in the bay,

how they fold their *alas* and then they dive
for ocean's bounty to keep them alive.

YEARS AT SEA

The graveyard between ocean and
crocodile enclosure offers a place

to sit and rest his lungs, air
sustaining meat with wings above

a stretch of sand unsullied yet
by Japanese earthquake detritus.

NO PUEDE VER

This oblique man, insect itches
up and down both legs, he

is partly here on the beach:
how little he really knows

of Japan, of earthquakes, of unseen
mosquitos, the flat of his hand.

NO IDEAS

Está reposando on this yellow deck,
sufficiently protected from sobriety,

ears attentive to abstract words,
he can't read the price on the bottle

to gauge how good all this is,
all this untoward restfulness.

EVENING SCULPTURE

Laila's sister teaches her arithmetic,
pulling her hair when she looks

across the street. Where the gringas
work the blender, drink the numbers

memorized from the book in the kitchen
where *las mujeres* come and go.

ORION'S BOY

Los pelícanos dive into *pescadores'* nets
because that's where the fish are.

Then the four men gather to free
and let fly, an astral version

of catch and release. Our sky here
records all of this in specks of fire.

MARINE LIFE

She sells sea shells by the
sea shore and she's in on

the joke. Come back *mañana*
he says, and she has more of them

than he could hope for, this
venera from the far ocean north.

5–0

His white plastic chair ten
metres from the touch line

at the *campo deportivo* became
a goal for the three-year-old

futbolistas behind him. How bright
they were, how drab the big pitch.

SOLUCIONISTA DEL REY

Wings beyond his language, *des-*
graciadamente, fold, and the fire

told springs from the sea, glints
for a moment and is gone, like

a simile into an immense la-
cuna no one will ever translate.

OR THE POT

How little he loves the world,
not the thing, but the idea.

A sweet hummingbird, for example,
smallest Buddhist on Earth, never

stays long enough for a complete
sentence, never counts the syllables.

ORIENTE

That frigate bird nipped that silver
fish and lifted that duck off his

feet from the hard wet sand, where
Japan may reach this coming

June, recall last year's tsunami,
a wharf at a time, a light bulb, too.

PSYCHE

His soul, if he still has one,
is softer on the edges, in

Melaque the gringos lock their
bicycles, hummingbirds stay away.

He remembers the Aztecs, how
butterflies indicate sexual flowering.

STOUT CORTEZ

Caterwauling radio next door, no
bird in sight but the boy in the yard

sweeping, as willing to say hello
as any teenager anywhere, hello

America, is it all settled? Did
those bastards get all the gold?

SO MUCH DEPENDS

That unfortunate duck that rimed
so nicely not at all turned out

to be a booby with white feet
that lately stand for comfort

beside a wounded pelican, now
they say, fed fish by this companion.

RENAISSANCE VERSE

At the cappuccino shop he
and a lone sparrow share bun

and icing, bird as quick in this heat
as any Philip in the snow.

He, though, will plod uphill toward
a well-fed, well-caffeinéd nap.

LAST DAY HOME

Por supuesto las campanas de la
iglesia son puertas de su sueño

in to this *agave* afternoon, plastic
chairs in sand, seabirds unaware

of his homeland, he honours these *Indios,*
how they have borne this European weight.

Acknowledgments

Thanks to Sam Weselowski, Erín Moure for her sharp eyes, ECW Press for permission to reprint *His Life: A Poem* (Toronto: ECW, 2000), Pierre Coupey for the cover image, and the team at Talonbooks.

Index of Titles and First Lines

This index treats each of the thirteen books collected in this volume as single poems, some of which are divided into sections. *Italicized* text denotes first lines, regular text denotes section titles, and CAPITALIZED text denotes poem/book titles. Sections titled with numbers alone are listed only by first line. *Baseball* and *Genève*, having no sections, are listed by title and first line only. Sections in *Irritable Reaching* are listed by title only. Ellipses indicate a continuing line that has been truncated for length in this index.

J

K

L